Praise for *Not Just a Soup Kitchen*

"A must-read for church leadership and individuals who sincerely desire to follow Jesus in service to those in need."

—*Rev. David W. Delaplane*
Former National Chairman of The Clergy Committee
Recipient, US Presidential Award for Outstanding Service on Behalf of Victims of Crime

"David Apple has a noble track record of showing mercy and serving 'the least of these.' Not that he would necessarily be happy with that expression because he instinctively sees such people made in the image of God and accords them extraordinary dignity as such. I find that one of the most winsome and characteristic elements of his ministry. He is a champion of those who are most easily overlooked, and like our Lord, reaches out to help them. This ministry of mercy has led to his passion to revisit some of the biblical texts relating to the diaconate, and he offers wise advice on how churches develop and utilize that significant office. You will find this work heartwarming and challenging. May God use it to His glory."

—*Liam Goligher, Senior Minister*
Tenth Presbyterian Church

"David's personal story of tragedy, hardship and brokenness shows how David was transformed through the powerful gospel of Christ and then called and shaped by God for the ministry of mercy and justice that he has pursued for the past years. As the story unfolds, he moves on to tell us how the ACTS ministry of Tenth Presbyterian Church was started and has grown to engage the least, the last, and the lost from the community surrounding the church. This book is a must-read for anyone who has been called of God to this kind of ministry. This is one of the most practical books on mercy and justice that I have ever read. I recommend it highly."

—*Bill Krispin, Former Executive Director*
Center for Urban Theological Studies and CityNet Ministries

"David Apple is a veteran from the front lines of the ministry of mercy. This practical and clear guide offers real-life wisdom gleaned from countless lives blessed through Christlike care. Through *Not Just a Soup Kitchen,* you and your congregation can be transformed as you partake of the spiritual nourishment offered here."

—*Dr. Peter A. Lillback, President*
Westminster Theological Seminary-Philadelphia

NOT JUST A SOUP KITCHEN

How Mercy Ministry in the Local Church
Transforms Us All

Dr. David S. Apple

PUBLICATIONS

Fort Washington, PA 19034

Not Just a Soup Kitchen
Published by CLC Publications

U.S.A.
P.O. Box 1449, Fort Washington, PA 19034

UNITED KINGDOM
CLC International (UK)
51 The Dean, Alresford, Hampshire, SO24 9BJ

Printed in the United States of America

ISBN (paperback): 978-1-61958-174-6
ISBN (e-book): 978-1-61958-175-3

CONTENTS

Introduction

The story of the Bible is one of eternal redemption. Of how God takes the trauma and brokenness of those He redeems and transforms them into gifts for His use in ministry. This book is the story of how God transformed my life—from a near-death skull fracture, childhood sexual abuse, hopelessness, marital betrayal, spiritual bankruptcy and thoughts of suicide—to today being the minister of mercy at a historical church in the heart of Philadelphia. It is also the story of Tenth Presbyterian Church's ministry of mercy and compassion and will serve as an instructional guide for diaconal ministry; empowering Christians who are starting new ministries in the local church.

Today, so many churches are comfortable following the practice of previous generations who didn't involve themselves in ministries of mercy. Many, today, are fearful of thinking "outside of the box" and lack vision and biblical direction. One small group at Tenth challenged that same attitude and because of that many others caught the vision. Wanting to feed the hungry, they asked the question, "How can our ministry be different from a soup kitchen?" Because of their actions, lives have been transformed and captives have been set free—both those outside the church and those in the pews. What would your church look like if you did the same?

Throughout these pages, you will learn about how people serve and what initially stirs up a person's heart for ministry. I hope you will be encouraged by their confidence for serving in areas that most Christians refuse to go. I hope, also, that you will be encouraged by a user-friendly framework for diaconal ministry and answers to several of the frequently asked questions (FAQs) on mercy and diaconal ministry I've received. Finally, I've included other resources that will benefit your ministry and your walk with the Lord.

1

A Journey from Death to Life

L ife is not easy for anyone. Growing up crippled and without hope, however, made life for me even more difficult. My journey has been filled with both pain and sorrow, grace and redemption; I've spent time in the valley, in the wilderness *and* on the mountaintop.

It was certainly not on my early agenda to suffer physically, emotionally and spiritually. But I suppose that is not what some in the Bible planned either—not Job, nor Moses, nor Joseph. Like Job, I experienced loss. I felt like everything was taken away. Like Moses, I was suddenly in the wilderness, wandering and seeking God's direction, wondering what would happen next. And similar to Joseph in Genesis 50:20, I was betrayed. Yet, God used it all for my good and the salvation of many. Other passages echo my story as well:

> "Though you have made me see troubles, many and bitter, you will restore my life again; from the depths of the earth you will again bring me up." (Ps. 71:20, NIV 1984)

> "I will repay you for the years the locusts have eaten." (Joel 2:25 NIV 1984)

There are occasions when, in a pivotal moment, everything changes—when God takes people's trauma and brokenness and transforms them into gifts for use in ministry. This book is partially the story of how God transformed my life after surviving a near-death skull fracture, childhood sexual abuse, teenage hopelessness, marital betrayal, spiritual bankruptcy and thoughts of suicide as an adult. This book is also the story of how I became the minister of mercy at a historical church in the heart of Philadelphia and how the church must continue its ministry of mercy and compassion to those suffering from their own trauma and brokenness.

How it began

I write through the eyes of someone who has been broken physically, emotionally and spiritually and who badly needed mercy and compassion. I am thankful for my parents, non-religious Jews, who were loving, compassionate, ethical and politically active, always fighting for the underdog and heavily involved in the civil rights movement. They gave me a good foundation and a concern for others. Life, however, would teach me so much more.

Impacts

At the age of five, my brother Michael and I were playing ball on the sidewalk as we very often did. I missed the ball (a rarity) and it went into the street. Michael recalls that I ran into the road after the ball just as a speeding driver hit me. Michael saw it all. He saw me lying under the back of the car and began screaming at the top of his lungs. He finally ran inside calling for our mom. She collapsed. Michael was both numb and shaking. I lay there, still and unconscious in the road, blood hemorrhaging from my ears, mouth and nostrils. My only movement was the involuntary spasm of one hand back and forth, back and forth.

That is how it all began for me. I was just a normal five-year-old boy, playing ball on the sidewalk with his brother. Then I wasn't.

I've been told that a neighbor gathered me in his arms, placed me in his car and drove me to Paterson (New Jersey) General Hospital. The doctors told my parents, "We're not sure that he's going to live. We'll have to drill holes in his skull to relieve the pressure." After this was done, the doctors said, "Your son is going to make it, but he is still in a coma." Several days later the doctor said to my mother, "Your son will live, but he'll never walk. We don't know what his life will be like." A week later, I woke from the coma and spoke four words—swearing, actually, at a male cousin. To my parents though, they were the most beautiful sounds in the world. I was alive. My left side was paralyzed; my right eye blinded. But I was alive.

I was alive.

Future recovery would include wheelchairs, heavy leg braces and hand braces. There would be more surgery and fifteen years of physical and occupational therapy at Kessler Institute in Orange, New Jersey, and with the Passaic County Cerebral Palsy Association. After many years, I was finally able to tie my shoes. Given my initial prognosis, this was a remarkable success.

A few years after the auto accident, I was at least twice sexually abused by my older cousin, Douglas. Was the fact that my first "post-coma" words were curses at him an indication that this abuse was ongoing? I never found that out. I didn't have the courage to talk about it for another thirty years. By then, Douglas was in a California mental institution, and when I spoke to family members, no one was aware of the abuse as I told no one when it occurred.

However, because of the abuse, I was not only physically crippled, but felt emotionally crippled as well—with scars that would not heal for years and years. I felt broken with absolutely no hope of ever being healed. I felt unworthy and believed also that I was no good. Most certainly, I felt abandoned by God (even though at the time I believed He didn't exist). I grew up to be a very angry, sarcastic, bitter and hopeless person.

Faith was nowhere on my radar.

Impacts

As a preteen and teenager, my only escapes were baseball and bowling. I followed my beloved Brooklyn Dodgers and my heroes Jackie Robinson and Roy Campanella. I always thought, *If they could make it, so can I.* As for bowling, this sport requires only one hand, and for many years I excelled and became a champion bowler.

At age sixteen, I finally fully recovered from surgery to lengthen my Achilles tendon. It was the first time since being hit by the car that I could stand upright and walk straight and run without tripping. My bowling had never been better.

Following a January snowstorm the next year, I was on my way to participate in the finals of the state bowling championship. Driving my dad's Volkswagen minibus, (a vehicle with the engine in the back) I suddenly hit an icy patch, spun around and sped across a three lane highway. Looking ahead I saw the rail, and feared I was going to die. Just then the minibus was hit by another car. It spun around again and threw me to the ground. Everything went black. Soon after, I opened my eyes where I lay on the shoulder of the highway, just inches away from the rear tire of the minibus. With the help of the other driver, I got up and as there were no serious injuries—I was just scratched, after all—got back in the car, which was running just fine, and drove home. Suffering only minor cuts and bruises, I said to myself, "Boy, I am lucky."

Good friends, good news

Around that time and for the next few years, several African-American Christians befriended me. We had a mutual friend, Jimmy, with whom I worked. It wasn't like I was their "project," a sinner to be saved. No, they just loved me and cared about me. They told me some crazy stuff about their Savior, Jesus—how He had lifted them out of the "ash heap and the dung pile" (Ps. 113:7, paraphrased) and richly clothed them in robes of splendor. I repeatedly responded, "Go away with that. I have no hope. There is no God. Leave me alone with this Jesus." But, then one day I met a man who was old, poor, blind, crippled and lived in a rat and roach infested apartment, who said that he was rich, whole and well. More and more, God brought me into contact with people who, though poor, said that they were rich. After years of fighting them off, finally I said, "These people may be crazy, but they have what I want."

I studied the Bible in the company of poor people and worshiped together with them at Northside Community Chapel, an inner-city Christian Reformed church plant (chronicled in the book *Chains of Grace* by Stan Vander Klay). I remember reading the Bible for the first time and believing that this was God's Word. This was after years of denying His existence and being totally ignorant of the truths contained in Scripture. I remember the first time I read the Exodus story. I knew the story but thought it was something the film director Cecil B. DeMille had made up for his film, *The Ten Commandments*. This was an "Aha!" moment for me as a new believer, to read the Bible and see that historically God had a plan to deliver His people and to save them from their sin, going all the way back to Genesis 3. I was beginning to believe what my new friends said about God—Father, Son and Holy Ghost. Yet, I still had some doubts. That is, until. . . .

Not again

I was driving down a narrow one-way street on my way to speak to the minister about my belief in Scripture, about baptism and about church membership. Suddenly a child dashed out in front of my car. Before I could step on the brakes, I hit him, sending the three-year-old boy skidding and rolling down the road before he stopped—motionless. I buried my head in my hands, horrified. I heard the mother scream and visualized my own accident many years before: me running out, getting hit by the car, people screaming.

The police and paramedics came, and I followed them to Paterson General Hospital, the same hospital I'd gone to. I waited in a state of shock and disbelief, asking myself, "Did I kill him? Oh no, Lord. Don't let him die." Finally the doctor came out and said, "I have good news. Edwin is okay. He is badly bruised, but he has no internal bleeding, no breaks or injuries. He'll go home in about an hour and he should be fine." That news was such a relief. And at that moment, without a doubt, I knew that Jesus Christ was my Savior. Just as God had saved Edwin's life just then, I knew He had saved me from physical death many years before. More importantly, I also knew that God had saved me from eternal death as well. At that moment, I knew that God had used a unique process of suffering to get my attention and had brought to me people who had suffered in a variety of ways, yet were victorious in Jesus Christ. I knew that I was saved for all eternity. God got my attention, and soon after I was baptized and made my public profession of faith. At that worship service, my pastor used the text from Isaiah 61, "The Spirit of the Lord God is upon me, because the Lord has anointed me to bring good news to the poor; he has sent me to bind up the broken-hearted, to proclaim liberty to the captives, and the opening of the prison to those who are bound; to proclaim the year of the Lord's favor" (61:1–2). I took that verse to heart—the Spirit of the Lord had anointed me to do something. He called me to bring the good news to the poor and to give spiritual sight to the blind. He called me to release the captives. But there were more changes to come.

Vocation and service

After praying and talking to many people, I was led by God to be a Christ-centered social worker, working for the government. While in college, I interned at my hometown welfare department in Paterson, New Jersey. Upon graduation I became an investigator and then a caseworker. With my hope in Christ and the knowledge of His mercy and grace, I could come alongside individuals who were suffering and offer material and spiritual resources to them and families who were impoverished and without hope. Even though government service restricted my use of Scripture and prayer, I decided early on to obey God's law rather than man's. I would ask those with whom I met, "May I pray or read Scripture with you?" If they said yes, I would. If not, that was okay too.

I went on to work for another government agency in crisis intervention and public advocacy. At the Action Now Center, I had the opportunity to help people navigate through the social service system in such a way that they would become independent of welfare or other financial needs and dependencies. But the biggest blessing was helping people become dependent on Jesus Christ in that process. And, although my supervisor warned me to keep my religious beliefs separate from my work, I sought—with my client's permission—to pray and read Scripture with those who came in for help. My boss would say, "You can't do this." And I responded with, "I can't not do this." For this reason, after five years, I was given an ultimatum: change, quit or be fired. I handed in my resignation and began working in, and eventually managing, my father's printing company.

This was one of many nudges by God; hints that a major shift in terms of what I would "do" with the rest of my life was underway. But not without more trials, of course.

Unanticipated changes

When I was twenty-seven, my former spouse and I separated. She left our home and I became a custodial single parent of three children ages six, four and two. I said, "I can do this. I'm a real man." I felt that I could take care of my kids, could work and could take care of myself, worship and grow in the Lord. And, I did. But, thirteen months later, upon my return home from vacation, I found that my former spouse, with the help of others, had moved herself in and moved me out of my home. Imagine coming home and finding someone who should not be there residing in your home. On top of that, imagine that they had removed all your belongings and stored them in the basement. That was an awful experience! After two weeks of being a stranger in my own home and sleeping on the living room sofa, I moved out. I took only my clothes, books, records and stereo.

Not wanting to put my children in a tug-of-war, I removed myself, got my own apartment and lived alone. I felt so much grief and loss. I stopped caring about myself. On nonvisitation days, I worked all day, came home and would consume liquor until I passed out.

This suffering and depression went on for about a year. In addition, my church attendance suffered, as did my relationship with God. I despaired of life and I felt suicidal. I was so miserable that I wanted God to take me and actually prayed that He would—I was too frightened to do it myself. The last time I drank to excess, I passed out, fell down, hit my head and woke up sometime later in a small pool of blood. I knew that I was in danger and might have died. I was so angry at myself and so sick and tired of being sick and tired with this sinful behavior that I screamed a Bible verse at God (as if He didn't know it). It was incredible. I looked up to heaven and yelled with a clinched fist, "You promised You wouldn't give me more than I could bear (see 1 Cor. 10:13). Well that's enough, I can't take it anymore!"

Imagine how I felt. This was such an astonishing "Aha" moment. As I listened to these words of Scripture, the truth of the verse hit me for the first time. It was true: God promised not to give me more than I can bear. He is faithful to me in the time of my temptation and trouble. He will come alongside me and give me a way of escape. I knew that I had wandered away from Jesus Christ for that full year, and I was scared of dying, and I could have died. I knew at that moment that I couldn't do anything without Him. I surrendered.

In that moment and the moments to come, I rediscovered just how merciful God is. He saved me after being hit by the car when I was five years of age and saved Edwin when I hit him. He saved me from eternal death when I was nineteen. He even healed the emotional scars from the sexual abuse. He brought me through loneliness and despair when my children were taken away and showed His faithfulness by returning them to me nine months later.

But the lessons were not over.

Getting my attention

In 1980, I married my lovely wife, Kate. Two years later, on Halloween night, Kate and I were driving to a family function. Streetlights lit up the dark road. Several cars in front of us stopped to let trick-or-treaters cross the street. We slowed down and stopped, too. The car behind us, however, did not. We heard the screeching of the brakes and then the sound of metal against metal as the speeding car driven by someone high on drugs slammed into us. I suffered a severe lower-back injury; Kate was uninjured.

God got my attention again. Not physically able to manage the print shop, I was out of work for four years. I wasn't producing anything and wasn't making any money. How empty I felt when those things—those props of job and income—were taken away. I saw that my self-worth was in my work, in what I produced, and in the amount of money I earned, but not in whom I was in Jesus Christ. I hit bottom again. Once again, I needed to look to things above. And I had all the time I needed, because I was on my back with severe chronic pain. One thing I could do was pray and read Scripture. In doing so, Job became my best friend—Joseph, Moses and Hosea too. I discovered God's presence in the wilderness with Moses, and dealing with tragedy with Joseph, Job and Hosea. I rediscovered the God who strengthens me and gives me hope. During those years, as never before, God revealed His mercy and grace to me and exposed my spiritual bankruptcy. He showed me that my identity is not in what I do or how much I earn, but in Him alone. I went from saying in anger, "Why are You doing this to me?" to saying with humility, "How are You going to use this for Your glory and my benefit?"

The answer to this question came when God gave Kate and me the opportunity to take biblical counseling courses at a messianic synagogue in Brooklyn. We attended for six weeks and after that, God opened the doors for me to go to Christian Counseling and Educational Foundation (CCEF) near Philadelphia for one and a half years.

Since the accident, I had been living with chronic back pain. After completing my studies at CCEF, I enrolled elsewhere—this time in the "low-back school" run by Kessler Institute (where I had therapy and surgery many years before). There I was taught how to temporarily abolish pain and teach new body mechanics to my muscles and limbs to further avoid pain. I prayed about the next step. When would I be physically ready to work? Where would God lead me? How would He use my new counseling skills, my experience working in the urban arena and that of running a business? For eighteen months I applied to fifteen positions in cities across the United States including bigger cities like Chicago and New York, and smaller ones such as Ames, Iowa and Redlands, California. There was also one position in Philadelphia that I really didn't want and didn't apply to, but my Kate (who I always listen to) said, "You know, God can't say yes or no about Tenth Presbyterian Church's Ministry of Mercy unless you apply." So I applied, and the rest is history. That was 1988. Since then, the ministry I direct, ACTS (Active Compassion Through Service), has sought to make Tenth Church a safe and welcoming place for all people to worship and know the

Lord—especially those who have previously been ostracized or stigmatized by churches.

Because of God's redemption and healing in my own life, and with the help of the church, I have been able to bring the same mercy, compassion and hope of God to others with the goal that they too might be drawn to Jesus.

And God absolutely draws people to Himself, but exactly how does He get our attention?

Our life experiences.

God uses our families, our rearing, our schools and our neighborhoods. He uses accidents and injuries and trauma, heartache, abuse, abandonment and failure. And yes, God even uses success to remind us that there is nothing in us that allows us to stand apart from Him. For everything we possess or experience comes from God's hand alone and He uses all our experiences for His glory and our benefit. His timetable is perfect, and His grace sufficient (see 2 Cor. 12:9). My favorite illustration of this is Genesis 50:20 where Joseph—betrayed and abused by his brothers—says, "As for you, you meant evil against me, but God meant it for good, to bring it about that many people should be kept alive, as they are today."

Serving with the grace I've been given

I can serve others because of my thorough understanding of how God has served me. When I think about the new life He has given me, I remember it with tears of joy and sorrow. It took me about fifteen years as a believer before I thoroughly understood God's grace. Before that, every time I looked in the mirror I saw someone ugly and unworthy. Have you ever had such a horrible feeling? I still saw someone who, because I had been abused, was no good and not worth saving. But that masked God's truth. I couldn't change the image that I saw, but I could remind myself that in Jesus Christ, I'm clothed with His righteousness, and all is forgiven.

Now when I look in the mirror, I see the redeemed person that God sees. There are old wounds, yes, but there are now scars, and the wounds are healed. The past doesn't hurt anymore. If you've suffered some form of abuse, you know it is like a truck dumping its load of stones on you. Life becomes difficult. And the long restoration process begins by removing one stone at a time, recognizing that God has the power to come alongside with a backhoe to take that entire burden of stones on Himself.

What prevents that from happening many times is that we don't give Him permission. Sinful pride has you and me holding on to things that hurt us instead of crying out to God for relief. But if we understand God's grace, know that we are forgiven and realize that the past is gone; we can look in the mirror with a new perspective as new creatures in Christ. Now when I view myself, I see the limp, I see a hand that still doesn't function well, I see a lip that does not go up on one side. But I know that despite the past injuries, I am whole. I am a recipient of God's mercy. I can be vulnerable with strangers and friends because I know who I am in Jesus Christ. I can be totally vulnerable because I know Jesus as the advocate who has come alongside of me, has gotten under my skin and has taken all my emotional baggage on Himself. I know Jesus saved me from sin and freed me to serve. God made me His instrument and gave me the heart of a servant.

2

The Heart of a Servant

My dad, a printer, had a phrase I'd hear often: "Why do I always have time to do things twice, but never have time to do things right?" I guess my philosophy, "Do it once, and do it right" has its origin in that. In life and ministry it is important that we know what we're doing (and do what we know). Best intentions are not good enough. Even our best intentions won't prevent the gravest of mistakes. Speaking of this, Joe Aldridge writes about a college graduate's best intentions in his book, *Gentle Persuasion*:

> Diploma in hand, he signed on as a farmer. Now a graduate of Aggie Tech, he was ready to follow in the tradition of his grand alma mater. He decided to grow chickens. Cranking up the John Deere, he headed out to the fields and planted his chickens head first in rows. They didn't do too well. But the Aggie wasn't one to give up easily, so he again fired up the John Deere and prepared the soil for a second batch, this time planting the birds feet first. To his credit, this crop kicked up dust for a little longer, but they, too, died. Failure was staring him in the face. Something was wrong! But, what? Suddenly it dawned on him that as an alumnus of Aggie Tech, he could write to the extension department, describe the problem,

and get a solution. With renewed hope, he sat down at the kitchen table and put his problem on paper. He finished his letter and popped it in the mailbox. Days later, a letter came addressed to him, from "Aggie Tech Extension Division." At last, he had his answer! Hustling into the kitchen, he slashed open the envelope and yanked out the note. It was short. "Dear Sir, please send soil sample."[1]

Clearly this farmer didn't know what he was doing and even his source for guidance was lacking. If we are going to plant the seeds of faith, talk the talk of faith and walk the walk of faith, we need to go to the right source for guidance and follow its instructions carefully.

One of the songs from the Broadway musical *My Fair Lady* gives us another incorrect model:

> The Lord above made man to help his neighbor,
> No matter where, on land or sea of foam.
> The Lord above made man to help his neighbor, but
> > With a little bit of luck,
> > With a little bit of luck,
> When he comes around *you won't be home*.[2]

This is certainly not biblical.

Proverbs 3:27–28 says it correctly, "Do not withhold good from those to whom it is due, when it is in your power to do it. Do not say to your neighbor, 'Go, and come again, tomorrow I will give it.'" Similarly, Galatians 6:10 says, "As we have opportunity, let us do good to everyone, and especially to those who are of the household of faith." This leads to three questions: Who is our neighbor? Where will we be neighbors? To whom will we be neighbors?

Who is our neighbor?

One Sunday, while walking down a sunlit street and admiring the marble steps of a brownstone, a Tenth Presbyterian Church member saw a green blanket nestled between the steps of a building. She would later say to her husband, "Before moving to Philadelphia I would have assumed the blanket had accidentally fallen while being aired outside. Instead I found myself looking around for the homeless person who slept on the street that night across from the church."

The areas where most of us live are areas of contrasts. There is wealth and there is poverty, there is joy and there is sorrow, there is laughter and there is mourning. The Center City Philadelphia area surrounding Tenth Presbyterian Church is a microcosm of these contrasts. One block from the church are condos for which people paid over one million dollars. Yet, sleeping in the alleys and eating from the rubbish containers are homeless men and women. According to the news, the poverty population of Philadelphia is increasing while the total population is decreasing. Schools have failed. The adult illiteracy rate is high. City shelters are filled to capacity. There is an increase in human need.

When confronted by needs, people exhibit a variety of attitudes. Some wonder whether the needy are worthy of help. Many call them the "undeserving poor." Many define for themselves just who is and who is not their neighbor. They say something like, "Be reasonable, God. We know we are supposed to help 'the unfortunate,' but just how far do we have to go?" They may quote Benjamin Franklin's proverb, "God helps those who help themselves," believing it is Scripture. They may even try to opt out by saying, "We're not good at that kind of thing. Compassion is not one of our gifts." Whatever excuse they make,

God's truth is that anyone in need is our neighbor. In *The Dea-cons Handbook*, Lester DeKoster says,

> Why waste time discussing how we will know who our neigh-bor is? Just go and be a "neighbor" to someone, to anyone, in need. Let the needy find his neighbor in you. Drop the talk. Cut the chatter. Take God's gifts of time, money, goods, talents, counsel, a listening ear, a helping hand . . . out there where someone can use them. To love your neighbor as your-self means simply to be a neighbor whenever and wherever you can.[3]

Similarly, Japanese theologian Kosuke Koyama says: "The question *who is my neighbor* should be replaced by *whose neigh-bor am I*. For one cannot know beforehand whom he will meet." The immediate sight of a neighbor in need demands a spontane-ous answer.[4]

In the Gospel of Luke, Jesus tells a story to make clear who our neighbor is. The hatred between Judea and Samaria had ex-isted for over 400 years because while the Jews had kept their purity during the Babylonian captivity, the Samaritans had lost theirs by intermarrying with the Assyrian invaders. In the Jews' eyes the Samaritans were mongrels. And, the Samaritans had built a rival temple which the Jews destroyed. In Jesus' day the hatred was very much ingrained. The rabbis said, "Let no man eat the bread of the . . . Samaritans, for he who eats their bread is as he who eats swine's flesh." The ultimate insult came in the Jewish prayer that concluded, "and do not remember them [Sa-maritans] in the Resurrection."[5]

The Good Samaritan

In that historical context, Luke's parable of the good Sa-maritan displays a cast of characters: the wounded man, beaten, robbed and left for dead; the robbers who saw this person, walking alone (and an easy target); the priest and the Levite, two "religious" men who saw the wounded man as unclean; and the Samaritan who saw the wounded man as someone worth caring about. There was also the scribe, an expert on Jewish law, to whom Jesus told the parable, and Jesus Himself.

The scene of this parable is the road from Jerusalem to Jericho, a notoriously dangerous road narrow and rocky with many abrupt turns. This gave robbers the advantage over unsuspecting travelers. William Barclay's commentary on Luke 10 tells us,

> In the fifth century. . . it was still called "The Red, or Bloody Way." In the 19th century it was still necessary to pay safety money to the local Sheiks before one could travel on it. As late as the early 1930s, H. V. Morton tells us that he was warned to get home before dark, if he intended to use the road, because a certain Abu Jildah was adept at . . . robbing travelers and tourists, and escaping to the hills. When Jesus told this story, he was telling about the kind of thing that was constantly happening on the Jerusalem to Jericho road.[6]

Jesus told the story of the good Samaritan to state clearly what neighboring attitude is right and pleasing to him. In the parable, the religious ones—those who were supposed to be close to God—showed that their hearts were far from the heart of God. The Samaritan—the one despised by the "people of God"—demonstrated that he and his values were close to the heart of God.[7]

The two who passed by the wounded man may have been aware, but didn't care. The priest had good "religious" reasons for ignoring the man's need. If the body was a corpse, and he touched it, according to Numbers 19:11, he would be unclean for seven days. To the priest, law and ceremony were more important than love and the suffering of others. The Levite too would take no risks to help this man. The Samaritan, "the one whom all orthodox good people of the time despised . . . was prepared to help—the love of God was in his heart."[8]

In his commentary, Matthew Henry shows the perception of the Jewish teachers in this matter. To Jews of Jesus' era, a neighbor was "one of their own." Gentiles were the enemy. Samaritans were similar to Gentiles, for they intermarried with pagans. Jews "exempted" all Gentiles from their neighbor obligation as they were not of their own nation and religion. He continues,

> They would not put an Israelite to death for killing a Gentile, for he was not his neighbour: and, if they saw a Gentile in danger of death, they thought themselves under no obligation to help save his life.[9]

Barclay's commentary states that the rabbis defined who a neighbor was. "To them, neighbors were only those who were fellow Jews. Some said that it was illegal to help a gentile woman in . . . childbirth, for that would only have been to bring another gentile into the world."[10]

In his book, *More than Equals*, Spencer Perkins states that Jews didn't see Samaritans as their neighbors. Samaritans were half-breeds. The Jews even believed that if a Jewish person's shadow touched a Samaritan's, the Jew would be contaminated and if a Samaritan woman entered the Jewish village, the entire village would become unclean.[11]

How we answer the question "Who is my neighbor?" today has a lot to say about our attitude to people who we consider different. Perkins states that it doesn't take much imagination for each of us to figure out who Jesus would use as an example of "neighbor" in our hometowns.

For an Israeli, how about the Palestinian? For an Arab, how about the Jew? For a rich white, how about a black welfare mother? For a poor white, how about a middle-class black who got where he is through affirmative action? For a white family, how about the new black or Hispanic family that moved in down the street? For all of us, how about the unmotivated, undisciplined, undeserved poor? Or an AIDS victim who contracted AIDS not through transfusion but through homosexual activity or intravenous drug use? Who would Jesus use as the neighbor if he were speaking to us?[12]

The parable of the good Samaritan shows us the difficult road to take and the difficult action to pursue. Jesus' parable says that our neighbors are those people we have the most difficulty loving. People's general concept of "neighbor" today is geographical. We think of those who live near us and are most like us as our neighbors. Using the word as a verb, we tend to only neighbor those with whom we are comfortable. Our presuppositions about others (those not like us) shape how we respond to them, if at all. As the priest and Levite, we do not want to risk "becoming unclean" by getting involved with the one injured or with someone representing an ethnicity we are taught in our homes to dislike (or fear).

I like to introduce myself to people on my block who I haven't met. We are from different backgrounds and ethnic cultures, but we all want the same things for our block: safety, peace and quiet, kindness, cooperation. Saying to them, "Hi, I'm David. I live across the street (or down the block)," breaks down a barrier to communication that was previously there. We were just friends who hadn't met yet. It makes for good neighbors. It takes work, however. I'm still trying to figure out how to love the neighbor whose car alarm goes off all the time and the neighbor whose parties spill over into street fights and our having to call the cops. But when there is a need, like when the child next door died, we respond with kindness and help as a good neighbor should.

I've heard the story of a wealthy woman who wanted to see how much love her son really had for those in need. He'd certainly spoken about it. So, she pretended to be a homeless woman and sat outside his place of business. She looked the part well enough as her son, when she asked him for help, rudely and abruptly berated her. The mother was horrified by his lack of concern for others and the abusive treatment he showed toward her. His was not a "neighborly" response.[13]

There are departures from this lack of concern, of course. I remember, as a teenager, attending a basketball game between my high school and another integrated school. During halftime I was assaulted by a black guy who, mistaking me for someone else, punched me in the face. Immediately five or six young black women surrounded me and said, "It's okay. We'll protect you. He won't bother you again." They rushed to my aid until the danger was past. They neighbored me.

They neighbored me

As a freshman in college, I needed a Samaritan-like neighbor. I was the one in the road. And that road led me to my first encounter with Christian mercy when my friend, Jimmy, introduced me to his friends from a small, inner-city mission in Paterson, New Jersey.

Of course years before, I was literally the one in the road. And while I survived, I was left with paralysis on my left side, blindness in my right eye, unable to walk and with the need for multiple surgeries. But our neighbors mobilized around me and my family. For hours every day, they helped exercise my left arm, hand and leg. They were determined, and within a year I had movement on my left side. Later I had enough strength to stand. My wheelchair was taken away, and I walked with heavy, ugly braces.

My atheist Jewish parents did all that could be done for me and more—everything, that is, except give me hope in someone greater than myself. Because of the injuries, I had deep scars and considered myself crippled for life. Self-conscious about how I walked and haunted by how I looked in the mirror, I was filled with self-pity, rage and despair. And if that wasn't bad enough, my hopelessness increased when I was molested. I remember feeling even more ugly and wounded and abandoned. Even after surgery and fifteen years of physical therapy those emotional scars would not heal.

But then I met Jimmy. We worked together in my father's print shop and all the time he would tell me about his Jesus, what Jesus had done in his life. I'd say "There is no God. I have no hope." That is, until he introduced me to his friends from the mission. A unique bunch of black men and women, they were poor. Some were even blind and crippled. Others were former addicts and prostitutes. They seemed to have nothing yet came alongside me and showed me the abundance of what they did have. The blind man said he could see, the crippled man said he was whole, the ex-addict said he was recovered, the former prostitute said she was pure. I met an eighty-six-year-old blind and crippled man who lived in a rat- and roach-infested apartment. As far as I could tell, he had absolutely nothing going for him. And yet, he taught me so much. Superficially he had nothing, but inwardly he said he had everything. His face shone with a love and joy I'd never seen before. "It's because of Jesus," he said. Here was someone who, in this lifetime, had suffered more than I had, and had been victorious over it.

These were my neighbors. They saw my spiritual and emotional poverty, my physical needs, and for four years loved my bitter, sarcastic self. As was my practice, I used words to hurt others. I would insult them—calling them winos, junkies, whores and worse. They'd ignore the insults. I would attempt to cut them with my words. They'd smile. I would taunt them about their former, sinful lifestyles. They'd laugh. I sought to be cruel in judging them. They responded with kindness—even the man in the wheelchair who I called "crip," and the guy I called "pie-face" or "handsome" because his face had been misshapen in an accident. They saw my neediness and inward pain, lived out a biblical model of mercy and led me to a saving faith in Jesus Christ. Jimmy and his friends acted just as the Samaritan who took a risk and destroyed his schedule through personal involvement with a needy person of another race and social class. They knew that being a neighbor to me was not an option; it was a command. They knew that the church exists for the benefit of others because it exists ultimately to worship and serve God.

The power of conversion

These neighbors showed me that deeds of mercy are bridges to Christ. As they had tasted the grace of God, they did not give up on someone like me. Their experience of God's grace made them live incarnationally. As they had been welcomed by God, they were able to be welcoming to others. The late Roman Catholic theologian Henri Nouwen states that nothing else but God's transforming power can turn a stranger into a welcomed guest. He says, "It is possible for men and women and obligatory for Christians to offer an open and hospitable space where strangers can cast off their strangeness and become our fellow human beings."[14]

In that context, God's love can convert our hostility into kindness and the stranger into a guest. Conversion to Jesus Christ means following His example of living our lives for others (see Phil. 2:3–4). Conversion implies a transformation—a complete change of attitude, with new eyes in which to see the needs of others. Conversion makes us turn our hearts and hands to those in need. Conversion involves neighboring those whom we've kept at a distance.

I have been reminded by God many times that I am required to be kind to the unlikable and unlovely—to show love to all. Since 1989, Tenth Church has hosted a Bible study with our homeless neighbors. Several years ago I was at the door greeting and welcoming our guests when I was confronted by a rather unattractive person—a tall, rugged-looking man in a bad wig wearing a red dress and high heels. I felt repulsed as I shook Tina's rough-skinned hand saying, "Welcome to Fellowship Bible Study." I said to myself, "I don't want this person here." God convicted me right on the spot. Hearing my own judgment of this guest, I immediately confessed and repented of my sin. No one should be barred from hearing the Word of God. And Tina was not barred. He felt a genuine welcome and continued to study the Bible with us for three years. He also worshiped with his Fellowship Bible Study friends in the evening during that time. Tina was arrested and imprisoned soon after this. We maintained contact with him, but sadly, never heard from him again after his release years later.

So the questions remain: Who is our neighbor? How are we doing as followers of Christ? Do we keep "those people" at arm's length? Do we ever look at those in need like they are inanimate objects and treat them as such? Jesus didn't. His attitude allowed Him to love others unconditionally. His neighbors were a reality to Him. He saw their needs, their worth and value as people created in the image of God (see Gen. 1:26). Jesus gave up the right to have His own way. He put down the need to get even. Jesus' love was lived out in a lifestyle where happiness was not dependent on getting what He wanted but in putting the interests of others above His own. His words for those who follow Him are clear in John 17:18: "As [the Father] sent me into the world, so I have sent them into the world." And in John 13: 34 He says, "Love . . . as I have loved you."

As we truly accept Jesus' love, mercy and grace, we are empowered to love our neighbors. Seeking the same intimate relationship He had with the Father makes us content with nothing but His divine nod of approval. Being a neighbor does not have to calculate results, but delights only in being able to serve. It is indiscriminate and has heard the call to be "servant of all." Jesus showed us that neighbors minister simply and faithfully because there is need. He showed us that neighborliness is a lifestyle. It builds bridges and opens doors to people. It turns hostility into hospitality. It turns strangers into guests. It heals and binds up the brokenhearted.

Earlier I quoted the *My Fair Lady* lyric, "When he [your neighbor] comes around, with a little bit of luck, you won't be home." When we turn to the Word of God and consider the example of Jesus, we learn that for us, when our neighbor comes around for help, with a little bit of grace we will be home. And we will welcome those in need.[15]

3

ACTS –
Active Compassion Through Service

Welcome . . .

To all who are spiritually weary and seek rest;

to all who mourn and long for comfort;

to all who struggle and desire victory;

to all who sin and need a Savior;

to all who are strangers and want fellowship;

to all who hunger and thirst after righteousness;

and to whoever will come—

this church opens wide her doors and offers her welcome in the name of the Lord Jesus Christ.[16]

During a bitterly cold night in 1982, a small group of parishioners from our historic church in Philadelphia, Tenth Presbyterian, was leaving the church building after

Bible study when they came across a homeless person sleeping on the front church steps. The encounter sparked a response in them that meeting physical needs should be a part of the church's mission. Tenth members were increasingly seeing the needs of street people in the area and eventually approached the church's Board of Deacons, asking for leadership in the fulfillment of the diaconal commission for ministry to the poor. Over time a vision grew and the deacons established monthly meetings for those wanting to minister to the city's needy. About a dozen people attended the first meeting, which was chaired by one of the deacons. This committee chose the acronym ACTS (Active Compassion Through Service) to represent the group's expanding vision of a holistic ministry to the homeless and others with needs.

It became apparent to this concerned group of Tenth Church members that the homeless needed an ally to speak to some of their needs. Seeing the homeless and hearing the public outcry for help was an incentive and encouragement for Tenth Presbyterian Church to do something.

The problems of homelessness are great, and the people who are homeless represent great need. They are the economically disadvantaged, the chronically mentally ill, the substance abusers. These include mothers and young children, young able-bodied men, elderly men and women, veterans and the disabled. According to a Temple University report approximately 50,000 families are precariously on the brink of becoming homeless each month.[17]

As one man stated, "It can happen. . . . All it takes is a job layoff, because the way the economy is, if a person is unemployed for a short time their life savings could be depleted in no time."[18]

And then "It is a 24-hour-a-day, seven-day-a-week struggle to survive the barrier that society has placed upon a homeless person."[19]

Who are the homeless?

Homeless persons have many labels attached to them. They are alcoholics, they are mentally ill, they are $5-a-hit crack users, they are $500-a-lid cocaine users, they are single mothers-never-married, they are abused spouses, they are unemployed, they are underemployed, they are a two-parent family temporarily without funds. They come from dysfunctional families. They are not religious and attend no house of worship. They are religious and are church members—perhaps a member of your church. But one thing is for certain. They, like us, were created in the image of God (see Gen. 1:26) and have the same physical, social, emotional and spiritual needs. That's the perspective we must have when serving them.

Here is the truth: those who are homeless are the *et cetera* and the so forth. They are the faceless that people pass by. They are the inheritors of a culture of poverty. Their lives are like a treadmill. They feel like they are going nowhere, and they can't get off. They feel powerless. They are the victims of economic and social injustice. They are the victims of sexual and racial discrimination. They are Asian, Latino, African-American and white. They are migrant workers. They may be illiterate though not necessarily so. They may have no job skills though not necessarily so. They have often grown up with a great deal of anger and aggression sometimes born from limited access to advancement or empowerment.

Many of those who are homeless have turned to many agencies for help—even churches—but believe that these organizations are all part of the problem. For some, living in an alleyway, an abandoned house or on a hot air vent above the subway, is the only home they know. Greg believed he was in heaven. In his prime location in Philadelphia's business district, he could panhandle a good $30 per hour. He "placed his pillow" above a vent with dry heat to keep him warm. His place was just outside a travel agency that had photos of exotic places in the window. And there was an awning that kept him dry when it rained. He thought he had it made, that is, until he was arrested for violating his probation. Prior to this he had many opportunities to enter a Christ-centered addiction recovery program and get his life together, but decided against it. Now, arrested, he was on his way to prison, where God was as present as when Greg lived on the street. In prison, he "messed around" with Islam for a while, but that soon became distasteful to him. And then he met Jesus and his life changed completely and we continued to minister to him and visit.

For hundreds, like Greg, there is no place to live. City shelters are too violent and the private shelters have no vacancies.

The bottom line? They are our neighbors and need help. Addiction recovery. Life skills. Job training. Affordable housing. A relief from the stress. To be treated with integrity and respect. To love life again. Tenth Presbyterian's ACTS ministry was created to help with all of this and more.

Getting started

ACTS' first official move into community ministries was modest: it established a fledgling food and clothing closet. Over time though, five committees were formed, in keeping with ACTS' holistic approach: food and clothing, adult education, community dinners, elderly visitation and family ministry.

ACTS launched an annual Thanksgiving feast for their home-less neighbors. Eventually, the Community Dinner became a monthly event. By late 1984, a statement of purpose was ad-opted officially affirming that "ACTS Ministries is a ministry of Tenth Presbyterian Church coordinated through the Board of Deacons."

While Tenth was committed to the spiritual, intellectual and relational growth of its members—and all others it was able to influence—new ministries with poor and homeless persons were definitely "outside the box" for this church of mostly profes-sionals. Tenth's membership rolls at the time indicated a highly professional membership. This is consistent with the records of the Presbyterian Historical Society which show the following:

> Between 1830 and 1848 sixty-seven identifiable males were admitted to membership—forty-seven of whom worked in the non-manual sector. Eighteen artisans and two watchmen accounted for the other twenty. After 1848, however, this mixture was decisively shifted toward the already dominant professionals and businessmen. Between 1849 and 1863 not one identifiable artisan or other manual worker was admitted to Tenth Presbyterian Church.[20]

In a 1998 survey of 705 congregants, Tenth Church mem-bers are employed almost entirely as professionals and business-persons. The percentiles representing the adult congregation, from high to low are: medical/health services (15 percent), homemakers (9.6), educators (7.1), managers/consultants (4.7), engineers (4.5), missionaries (4), musicians (3.7), architects (3.3), attorneys (2.6), insurance (2.8), marketing-advertising (2.8), computer specialists (2.1), social workers (1.8), counsel-ors (1.8), accountants (1.7), bankers-investors (1.3) and artists-graphic designers (1.3). Twenty-eight different vocations totaled less than 1 percent, and 7 percent of Tenth members are retired. The ethnic makeup of the church at that time was 84 percent Anglo and European, 7 percent African-American, 8 percent Asian and 1 percent other nationalities.

When I came on board as Tenth's director of Mercy Ministry, the church was in the middle of its transition into a vibrant ministry outside the walls of the church. Today, it's not newsworthy that the poor; homeless; and working, middle and upper classes worship and serve together. Imagine who you would see sitting side by side. There in a pew are an opera singer, a homeless man, a businessperson and an ex-offender and his wife. Other pews have a similar representation of neighbors. All who wish to worship are welcomed. None are excluded. The same is true in our homeless outreach. You would see serving together an array of Christian servants: a pastor, a shelter resident, a man who served twenty-two years in prison, a teacher, fireman, short-order cook, college professor and a person on fixed income. They are black, white, Asian and Latino—the same as those we serve. This is normal at Tenth, a church known as a place of hospitality and care—for anyone in need.

Ministry context

Tenth's ministry context—Philadelphia, the City of Brotherly Love—is filled with history and growth, as well as challenge and need. This is typical of any urban setting with a population exceeding one million.

Tenth Church is in the heart of Center City, Philadelphia's downtown, and has a history that extends as far back as 1828, when railroads were still in the future and Andrew Jackson was president. It is a congregation of the Presbyterian Church in America (PCA), which it joined in 1981. Tenth holds to the classic formulations of Presbyterian theology that grew out of the Reformation,[21] which include *responding to certain needs by putting beliefs into practice locally*. We've been doing that for some time now. As an example, several years ago, a new ministry was developed when a federal prison was being built near Tenth. The new ministry focused on the needs of prisoners and their families.

Tenth in brief

Tenth operates a variety of ministries in addition to their mercy ministries. It provides the more traditional church programs for children and youth, of course. In addition it has a children's music school, neighborhood preschool and play group, medical campus ministry, college ministry, women's ministries, church-planting ministry and local urban and overseas missions. It also started and supports a classical Christian high school which shares its facilities. Tenth welcomes about 1,800 people each week at its three Sunday worship services. The church is committed to expository preaching, a network of fellowship groups aimed at meeting individual needs, a program of Christian education to promote the spiritual growth of its church family and, in cooperation with other Christians, an evangelistic outreach in word and deed to its city and the world beyond.

Tenth on mission

As I noted earlier, Active Compassion Through Service (ACTS) is a ministry presenting the gospel of Jesus Christ to the whole person—physical, mental and spiritual—and utilizing the talents and resources of Tenth's congregation. ACTS is concerned and directly involved with the spiritual needs of many poor and homeless persons. The second Sunday

Community Dinner Ministry provides a banquet and a worship service. Three Fellowship Bible Studies meet weekly and the ministry is also a sponsor for recovering addicts who have completed Christ-centered drug rehabilitation programs. And more vulnerable people find support, acceptance and healthy relationships through the Bridge Builders' ministry luncheons. The Nursing Home Ministry provides worship and regular visits to nursing home residents who otherwise receive few visitors. The Prison Ministry holds several weekly Bible studies for over fifty male and female inmates at the Federal Detention Center. In Philadelphia's Juvenile Justice Services Center, ACTS offers workshops for juvenile offenders on HIV/AIDS, anger management, sexual abuse, dealing with stress, asthma, sickle cell anemia, childhood diabetes, relationships and self-care. It also supports Christian and other Juvenile Services staff by meeting with them weekly for Bible study and prayer (more about these last two in the chapter, "You Don't Have to Reinvent the Wheel"). In the past, a Tutoring Ministry served thirty-five children a year from a local housing development (the high-rises have since been torn down). And divorced and separated men and women found support and acceptance in our Bridge Builders recovery ministry.

So yes, we are so much more than a soup kitchen.

All of ACTS Ministries are based on volunteers' involvement, relationships and trust. Their commitment to be involved shows their concern, and their genuine hospitality to our guests establishes this trust. If there is no trust then there are no listening ears, and, therefore, no ministry. In a world of phoniness and religious charlatans, each volunteer shows that she or he is genuine. They show themselves "neighborly."

Neighborhood Tutoring Ministry

The Tutoring Ministry existed from 1992-2007, serving children who resided in the former Martin Luther King Housing Plaza, a South Philly public housing development noted for its high crime rate, drug abuse, drive-by shootings and despair. In 2007, the high-rise apartments were slated for demolition by the city. We attempted to continue our ministry with our students, but as demolition drew near, all our families were moved and scattered throughout the city. Communication with them was difficult, and follow-up was limited. It was a transitional time for several leaders who also moved away. But, within a few years, Tenth's South Philly church plant, Grace and Peace, picked up the mantle and began tutoring neighborhood students.

The thirty-five children who participated each school year were enrolled in grades two through ten. But tutoring was only one part of the ministry. The most critical part was the establishment of godly one-on-one relationships between tutors and students that have lasted for many years. Many tutors committed to spending time together as big brothers or sisters to their students. The majority of children participated for several years. This continuity was vital in the lives of children who lived in poverty and in close proximity to the evil of drugs, violence and early death. It was also vital to the Christian tutors who were shown "the other side" of life such as they have never known it. There are some adults who no longer tutor yet still have relationships with their former students. One participant of seven years was the first in her family to graduate high school and then go on to graduate from college.

In addition to academic preparation, activities were provided for the students, individually and in groups. These ranged from playing sports to taking neighborhood children to amusement and theme parks. Some kids just hung out with their tutors. The most important thing to happen was that children came to know Christ. They recognized that our work with them was intended to be long-term, spiritually and otherwise. We hoped to prevent future homelessness, offer alternatives to drug abuse, offer friendships that the world cannot give and offer eternal life in Christ. Most of these children were unchurched. Even though there were three churches within sight of the projects, they had no contact with our families. So the more time tutors spent with their students, the greater the relational bond that grew between them. This encouraged trust between the parents and tutors, which helped foster stronger ties to Tenth Church as well.

Trust is a critical first step in establishing relationships with those we want to serve. When we, as "church folk," meet for the first time those whose experience with church has been negative—or who have a distorted image of God—they wonder if we will be different. Many wonder if we will treat them in a caring or brutal manner. So, when condescension and judgment are expected, we instead show love and compassion. We have to show that we are an alternative to what the world provides. When we have the opportunity to do good, we do it.

Bridge Builders

From 1990-2010, ACTS ministered to divorced or separated men and women, with or without children, through recovery seminars and support groups. The ministry provided support for those whose marriages had died and who experienced the same stages of death and dying that widows and widowers go through—anger, bargaining, depression, acceptance and forgiveness.

Our divorce recovery seminars were held in May and November, using the series, *Building Up the Castle That Has Fallen*

Down. With discussion groups, the seminar consisted of a total of fourteen hours of intense subject matter dealing with the grief process of separation and divorce. Six sessions focused on *Dealing with the Shock, Dealing with Your Former Spouse, Being a Single Parent, What About New Relationships, Forgiveness* and *The Process of Spiritual Growth*. We trained small group facilitators who, themselves, had experienced divorce and recovery. It was important for our guests to know that the facilitators were genuine when they said, "I know how you feel." In fact, each facilitator set the pace of discussion by briefly sharing his or her journey through the grief process. The seminar was open to anyone who had experienced the death of a relationship by separation, divorce or broken engagement. Seminar attendees came from Tenth, other churches, and those who did not attend church. Support groups followed. The feedback we received included such comments as, "I was really blessed by the seminar. I thought I was all alone in my pain. Listening to other people's stories really helped. Thanks!" "I appreciated having a sensitive facilitator who has been there." "I wish this seminar could have been available to me years ago. It would have prevented me from experiencing a lot of anger, hurt and anguish."

The goal of the ministry was restorative. BridgeBuilders sought to show that God is not judgmental toward the one who is separated or divorced but is merciful and understanding. Also, the diaconate was taught how the church can minister to this group by shepherding the hurting, reestablishing relations with the "new" family, integrating the family into the body life of church, providing child care for a "time out," providing meals, creating new extended families and watching out for children's special needs. Because of that training, more work has been done to integrate people into the body life of the church with greater recovery occurring through healthy relationships.

In 2010-2011, a number of our facilitators moved away or remarried. This directly affected our ability to put on recovery seminars. Since then Bridge Builders has broadened its reach by holding a monthly "luncheon and lecture" series for all comers on such topics as *How to Deal with Suffering* and *Dealing with the Enemy.* This has brought healing of emotions and encouraged relationship building by those who attend. Currently, there are discussions to renew recovery seminar efforts with new facilitators.

Nursing Home Ministry

This ministry serves two nursing homes in Philadelphia: Penn Center for Rehabilitation in University City and Powerback Rehabilitation in Center City. Three Sundays per month members of Tenth provide worship and visitation to the residents. Many of the residents receive no other visitors. The goal is to establish relationships with residents, provide friendship and hope to those who are lonely and offer salvation to those who do not know Jesus.

During the worship services, several volunteers bring the gospel. These include ministry leaders and seminary students. Children who play musical instruments regularly attend and participate in the service. Other volunteers sit with our guests, many of whom are in wheelchairs. The volunteers are encouraged to bring the blessings of touch, kindly spoken words and songs to our guests. The ministry uses extra-large-print hymnals for our guests, although most of the songs are familiar to them.

Some of the "fruit" evidenced from this ministry are the long-term relationships our volunteers have developed with some of the residents. As is true for all of the ministries of

ACTS, the formal programs provide the primary introduction for relationships and friendships. In addition to the more formal services, the volunteers may visit or correspond with a resident at any time.

One incident occurred when a volunteer was sitting next to a resident who, early in the worship service, was moaning in pain. Later, during the singing of "Amazing Grace," the volunteer held her hand. Almost immediately, the resident sat up in her chair and began singing. The words seemed to distract her from the present pain to remind her about a joyful refrain that she may have been familiar with in the past. This transformation changed the attitude of the volunteer who now knew how important this ministry was.

One other life-changing event occurred after a worship service had ended. As the leader was leaving the dayroom, a resident called out to him from her room. She related how she had been unable to dress herself and did not attend the service. She asked if he had a few minutes to speak with her. He did not stay a few minutes, but stayed much longer and gave her his entire sermon message. Following this she asked to receive Christ as her Savior. They prayed together and the leader left her with the hope of meeting again soon.

Later that night she passed away into the arms of Jesus.

The Nursing Home Ministry is a way for Christians to make themselves available to be used by God for a measurable amount of time with opportunities that can have eternal consequences.

Community Dinners: Not a soup kitchen

Every month people call and ask if they can help at our "soup kitchen." I have to explain that ours is a Christian ministry of hope and hospitality. The monthly Community Dinner Ministry is an alternative to the impersonal soup kitchen. In fact, it is a banquet for up to 120 of our poor and homeless neighbors. The ministry begins with our guests worshiping and then dining with church members whose sole ministry is to sit, eat and talk. When our guests arrive in the dining room, they immediately look for a familiar host who is assigned the same table each month. At that point there are pleasant greetings across the hall, and then people exchanging handshakes or hugs. The host's job is simply to practice hospitality, encourage conversation and make our guests feel welcome. Their job is to enter into relationships and to nurture those previously established.

The dinners encourage friendship evangelism, urban style. Our goal is simply to be available for God to establish relationships with our guests. Many workers who work and/or reside near Tenth invariably have contact with the guests who frequent the parks and streets nearby. Because of the introductions made at the dinners, relationships with our guests continue along with ministry and long-term friendships.

Each month, one of the six church parishes "sponsors" the dinner. A delegation of its members helps with setting up, preparing food, hosting, serving or cleaning up. There is something for everyone to do. Families with children are pleased to help set up the tables and chairs. Small children are able to participate by putting out tableware, napkins and Bible tracts. The food and drinks are served restaurant-style by youth groups from urban and suburban churches. This provides their teens with an unintimidating introduction to homeless persons, persons they speak with as they serve. You won't find this interaction at a soup kitchen—nor the transformations that take place in many lives. Our guests sense that we and the ministry itself are uniquely different from other churches and return again and again. They come back to study the Bible and worship too. Parish and youth group members note how the dinner is beautifully orchestrated and tables decorated (students at a local alternative high school provide table decorations each month). More importantly, their attitudes about these neighbors are changed. One parish member commented, "I can't figure out the guests from the hosts. They look the same." Such a telling statement about men and women with the same needs, desires and hopes.

When the Community Dinner is over and as the guests are leaving there are lots of smiles and hugs, and some hosts arrange to meet guests during the week for fellowship and Bible Study. Still others will attend a discipleship group, called Aftermath, which meets after the dinner. This is for men and women who want to learn more about Jesus' saving faith and how He can assist their recovery from drug addiction and transform their lives for all eternity. Because of the relationship and trust they established with Tenth's followers of Jesus, they are seeking similar intimacy with Jesus Himself. You won't find that at a soup kitchen.

Fellowship Bible Study: Providing further help

This thrice-weekly Bible study consists of a group of Tenth Church members and homeless, addicted men and women. It began in 1989 as an outgrowth of the relationships established in the Community Dinner Ministry.

While the dinners are the first point of contact, Fellowship Bible Study provides the longer-term help to bind the hearts of those who struggle with the inner turmoil of hunger, homelessness and addiction to alcohol, crack cocaine and other drugs. It seeks to rebuild lives through long-term relationships, referrals to Christ-centered addiction recovery programs and restructuring lives through Christian discipleship.

Jimmy used drugs for thirty-five years. He sought our help and entered one recovery program after another. His pattern was to stay a month or two, leave and go back into his addiction. He needed help, but wanted to be independent even more. He wanted to be in control of his life, but two incidents showed how out of control his life really was. He nearly lost his toes to frostbite sleeping in his car one winter. And he came close to death after being stabbed in the chest in a crack house. These episodes brought him to the realization of his true condition. He returned to us for help and eventually surrendered. His repentant spirit encouraged us to do everything we could to help. Jimmy entered a long-term program, came to a saving knowledge of Jesus Christ and reconciled with his family. He moved out of state to be close to them and became a member of a Bible-believing church.

Wilma benefited from being a part of our ministry. She'd done time in prison for murder. After serving her sentence, she became homeless and addicted on the streets of Philadelphia. She attended Fellowship Bible Study regularly but only wanted to feed on our physical food, not our spiritual food. She refused any help to deal with her addiction and lifestyle. Seven years later, she was arrested for stealing and was incarcerated once again. This time she acknowledged her brokenness and asked for help. Clean and sober, she was spiritually hungry, requested a Bible and fed on it, and God transformed her life for all eternity. We corresponded and spoke during her incarceration. Years later, when she was paroled, she returned to Philadelphia and became a member of a church with good Bible teaching.

The strengths of this ministry are that people coming out of addictive lifestyles are being redeemed and discipled. Many become members of Tenth and other churches. Once again the ministry demonstrates the transforming power of Jesus Christ to "set the captives free" from addictions to drugs and more, and has a redemptive influence on the families and neighborhoods. We make Christ real, make our church more credible to our neighbors, and make an impact on people's lives inside and outside Tenth Church.

Any church can reproduce similar ministry outreach. The dinners began with one invitation to shelter residents and a few cooks and servers. Now hundreds of people and multiple churches are involved. My involvement leading Fellowship Bible Study began with no one attending—homeless or otherwise. I was disappointed and asked myself, "What did I do wrong?" Yet, I was not discouraged. Because I knew God's faithfulness in the past, I trusted Him to be faithful in the present and future. So, I prayed over every empty chair for the person God would put there. And in the twenty-four years since then, He has done the rest. Answering the prayers, He has brought the people to sit in once empty chairs. He has made the ministry come alive and has changed lives.

How mercy ministry can come alive for you

The founders of the ACTS wrestled with a name. In the beginning, they wondered what they should call the new ministry. What they finally decided upon were ideas based on Scripture that could easily be put into practice. This reproducible model stands for the following:

- **Active**—James 2:26 states, "Faith apart from works is dead." ACTS takes the Great Commission seriously to go (to urban Philadelphia and beyond) and tell others about God's plan of salvation and transformation. ACTS workers share the gospel while imitating Christ and His love for those around us.

- **Compassion**—In love, God draws us to Himself. God showed us compassion in a tangible way when we weren't even interested (see Rom. 5:6). This love compels us to share with others the peace and purpose we have found in Christ. The Holy Spirit, in His power and love, enables us to love needy persons who live around the place where we live and worship.

- **Through**—God has given our body of believers gifts, talents and resources. ACTS through these reaches out to the community in mercy ministry.

- **Service**—The needs in the Philadelphia urban area are great. So are the needs near you. What better way to respond to God's gift of love than by giving your time, energy and yourselves in service. You can do this by listening, mobilizing, training and multiplying.

Listen

One critical ingredient toward developing mercy ministry is church leaders listening to their members. What are the needs they see? How do they wish to serve? In our case, Tenth's leadership not only listened to concern about our poor and homeless neighbors, they also helped to facilitate the early stages of ministry. In 1987, the deacons commissioned their own task force to examine the social services of the church, survey the community and determine how needs could be met. The task force recommended the hiring of a Mercy Ministry Director.

What is your passion? What particular needs tug at your heart? Is it the poor, the stranger, homeless persons, immigrants, abused spouses, sex trafficking? How many others share your burden? Bring it to your leaders and pray for God to direct your (and their) steps. Be confident in showing what you envision, how your plans will work and how your ministry can make a difference in the life of your church and community. In our case, one small group at Tenth had a vision for doing mercy, prayed about it and brought it to the attention of the deacons and elders.

Mobilize the members and offer hospitality

One of my goals in ACTS was to encourage congregational members to become more mercy-minded. This is a critical part of expanding the work of mercy ministry in your church. Use bulletin announcements and blog articles on mercy and justice to create awareness of needs and volunteer opportunities. In addition, expand your focus by encouraging members to network with other churches, missions and agencies. Use a portion of the worship service as a window into local needs and the growing vision the church has to meet those needs. At Tenth, we developed a "Living Church" segment about ministries that make a difference and how members can get involved (along with display tables for more information and sign-up). Seize every opportunity to highlight the biblical mandate to love the needy with God's compassion.

Leaders, ensure that the church's ministry isn't limited to ordained professionals who do most of the work. Encourage members to recommend new ministries. Pray for them and cheer them on to good work. Create opportunities for brainstorming with your members. Empower them to take action. Think what your church would be like if their actions succeeded and more members used their gifts and talents. Equip them by providing the tools and the affirmation they need.

Train people to serve smart

Over my many years of ministry, I have helped people to serve "smarter and more effectively." Through formal training and articles written in the church bulletin and websites, I have taught how to deal with manipulative people and "tyranny of the urgent" situations, as setting safe limits is vital. People who serve in ministries of mercy need a sense of balance in order to help others and cause themselves no harm. Our Lord tells us to do our best and to serve in a way that is pleasing to Him (see 1 Cor. 10:31) and that means being realistic and having common sense. Remember who really changes people and causes their spiritual transformation. Not you. If your efforts don't appear to make a difference, remember that God is not finished.

Recently, I received an e-mail from a formerly homeless man whom I discipled. Three years prior to this he joined the church, but subsequently "fell off the edge of the earth." During that time no one had seen him or knew of his whereabouts. In his e-mail he expressed a repentant spirit and he asked to speak with me.

The following week we met for a couple of hours during which time he shared candidly his tale of woe (which included an attempted murder on his life) and his desire to return to Tenth and Fellowship Bible Study. What he wanted most, however, was to recover the personal relationship with Christ that he had thrown away. All of this was very difficult for him as he felt that God would punish him for his actions and that Tenth would not welcome him back. What a wonderful time we had discussing the parable of the prodigal son!

A week later he also had a wonderful time worshiping with us and studying the word with his friends at Fellowship Bible Study. All he can do now is praise the Lord because God hadn't given up on him.

Multiply

ACTS has been happy to multiply our ministry by partnering with local churches. Our ministry's "on the job training" provides them with skills to reproduce similar ministries in their own communities. Out-of-state churches send teams to learn the "how and why" of our ministry in order to put them into practice. And we have workshops and seminars throughout the year at Tenth and elsewhere. In addition, Tenth is committed to multiplying mercy ministry in the city by empowering churches and church plants to have ministries of their own. With that commitment, Tenth supported a regional outreach called *MercyNet* and I was asked to direct this ministry for one year, with Tenth both providing my salary and giving me a leave of absence from other responsibilities. ACTS and Tenth have also been actively multiplying urban and mercy ministry nationally with the Christian Community Development Association and other organizations and churches throughout the United States where I have led workshops and taught on mercy ministry.

You also can help multiply ministry. What is your ministry expertise? Where can you help apply it elsewhere? What are other churches doing successfully? Can they help you or use the gifts and talents of your members in ministry?

We all desire to see church members—regardless of age—engaged in serving others. Teens serve all the time in our homeless outreach, from food prep to being wait-staff and engaging in conversation. Sunday school children help with the nursing home ministry and make the residents smile. One of our best prison volunteers began his ministry at the age of eighty-two. From the cradle to the grave, we train, mobilize and multiply ministry.

Evidence of transformation

One of the major successes we've seen in our ministry is the way God has transformed our congregation. In 1988, if a homeless guest sat in worship, members would have abruptly moved to another pew. Today, I see people not cringing or moving away, but greeting and welcoming them. God has done an incredible work in changing hearts, even mine. Early on, I wanted to beat people up with Scripture when they acted rudely and un-Christlike to our guests. I have had to trust God to work in one person at a time—even me. Through mercy, He has helped to change the paradigm of the church. It has been a lengthy process, and may be compared to turning an ocean liner around, yet God has done the work by changing hearts and empowering leaders.

Be patient with the process. During one mercy training seminar a diaconal leader lamented to me that it was ever so difficult to get the elders (and some deacons) to understand the need for a mercy ministry at his twenty-year-old church. He asked, "How can we convince them?" "You can't," I said. While we want to see change, there is no quick fix. It takes a long time. The question to ask is, "What do you want the church to look like in five, ten and twenty years?" Then, in answer to the question, begin preparing the next generation and future generations to be those hoped for servant-leaders. Equip hearts and minds. One other thing I said was, "Your church is only twenty years old. Tenth was one hundred fifty-five when it developed its mercy ministry."

Other signs of transformation

In the past, guests of our mercy ministry were treated unkindly by some church members. There was hostility. One shared, "They should go to a mission, not here." Today, our guests are welcomed. Attitudes have changed. According to another member, "ACTS is our way of meeting needs and living out the gospel of Jesus Christ. It is a natural reflection of our own faith in Christ. It helps us connect good news and good deeds." And, those who were not welcomed in the past now say, "ACTS is a place to go for hospitality, to be treated with dignity and to have physical, spiritual and emotional needs met. Tenth is a welcoming place to worship."

What happened with ACTS and Tenth could happen in your congregation. God is in the business of transformation. Where is He leading you to engage volunteers interested in serving others? How is He leading you to provide or receive training in the journey to love, accept and serve the impoverished?[22]

Who are "the homeless"?[23]

The homeless are often stereotyped as being bag ladies and addicted men. The following is a quick look at who they really are:

The Faces of Homelessness

I am a substance abuser: I have a sixth grade education. I have used drugs on and off since I was 10.

I have never worked. I am a high school graduate. I started drinking when I lost my job—and have not stopped. I am a Vietnam veteran. I started smoking dope during a firefight in Danang. I fought in Iraq and Afghanistan. Dope and post-traumatic stress disorder have kept me out of work and out of home.

I have an MBA from Harvard. I once snorted coke for fun at a party then I used it every day. I feel like my brain cells are burnt out. I can't perform my job.

I am a single father. I began drinking when my wife left me. My children have been taken away by the state. Life has no meaning. I seek escape. I want help. I can't find any. I used to receive public assistance and I drank or smoked it all up. Now I refuse monetary help—I can't trust myself. There is emptiness in my life. I have no hope.

I am a single mother. My mother is a single parent. I don't know who my father is. I had my first baby at 14. I am the third generation of my family on welfare. I have little schooling and no job skills. My son has developmental delays from eating lead-based paint. I am attending school for computer programming. I hope my daughter will not be on welfare when she grows up!

I am an abused spouse. As a child I was sexually abused by my father. Two months ago I was emotionally and physically beaten—raped—and abandoned by my husband. I won't trust men. I am afraid all the time. I have lost my support groups. I am in therapy. I hope my children survive.

I am underemployed and unemployed. I have a sixth grade education. I work odd jobs, odd hours. I don't earn enough to pay an affordable rent.

I have a high school diploma. I work two jobs, 16 hours a day. I sleep in a shelter which has a savings plan to help me get my own place. I am HIV+.

No one will hire me in my field. I have a Master's degree. I worked as a consultant in a prestigious design firm in Los Angeles and came east for a job that did not pan out. I've used up all my savings. I'm working odd jobs too. Things are really rough.

I am mentally ill. I was released from Byberry—Philadelphia State Hospital—when the State government was cutting its budget. My family doesn't want me. I'm frightened. I've lost my support group. I don't know what to do.

I am temporarily without funds. My wife and I lost our home and all our possessions in a fire. Or we were evicted after I lost my job due to illness. Or we are homeless because all our money is going for our son's heart surgery. We can get help from social service agencies if we can just get an apartment. Our families can't afford to take us in and they're crowded already. We are on 16 waiting lists for housing.

4

People and Choices – Serving the Addict

Little Joey was a drug addict who hated his life and lost it to crack cocaine, cheap wine and vodka when he could afford it. He was a member of Fellowship Bible Study for eight years. Joey rarely missed the study and when he showed up he was always clean, sober and clear-minded.

Joey wasn't an easy person to get to know and not too many FBS leaders really knew what made him tick. He never shared his deepest concerns with anyone. Nevertheless, he was pleasant and friendly and enjoyed being at the study. We liked him and he liked us.

Like many of our homeless and drug-addicted guests, he had an incredible database of the King James Bible and could quote chapter and verse without error. If I wanted to know where a particular verse was I would ask Joey. But he didn't know Jesus and he continued in his addiction—drinking alcohol and smoking crack.

The next winter was brutally cold and Joey was in and out of shelters, sometimes sleeping outside. We worried about him and tried to get him to enter a Christian recovery program. He said he wasn't interested. Then tragedy occurred. One night in December he was found frozen to death with an empty bottle of vodka in his hand. We grieved over his passing, not knowing what went through his mind that night or whether he had come to saving faith in Christ before he died.

*   *   *

Tom hated his life and what he'd become: addicted to alcohol, heroin, marijuana, crack and other mind-altering drugs.

Tom was born in Paterson, New Jersey. He grew up with three brothers and two sisters. When I spoke with Tom about his early life, he said, "Life seemed to be great, but a closer look would show that my family was dysfunctional and messed up." He was reared in a two-parent home, but his mother and father were both alcoholics who left the children, as Tom states, "unmanaged and unmanageable." Tom stopped going to school at the age of twelve. By that time he was a drug addict and was wandering away from home. Tom says that he called it "adventuring" but the court system called it running away from home. He soon found himself in shelters, institutions, jails, becoming very knowledgeable about "evil ways."

I actually met Tom for the first time in 1966, the year after my public profession of faith. I served in my church's "Summer Workshop in Missions" working with a small group of neighborhood kids. Tom was one of those children. I would not discover this fact until the early 1990s when I interviewed Tom for placement in a Christian rehab facility. It was a standard application and included information on place of birth and any church affiliations. We discussed how we came from the same town and spent a lot of time reminiscing about Paterson. Then we talked about early churchgoing. Tom shared where he grew up, which was the Christopher Columbus apartments (called, "the Projects"). When I shared that my church was just two blocks away, he asked what church that was. And when I told him it was Northside Community Chapel, he said he attended their vacation Bible school. More questions, more discussion led to the fact that he was in my class!

For years Tom was "in" his addiction but would not come to Tenth Church for help or anything else. It was the care of a Tenth member that changed that. Bess lived near where Tom "put his pillow" (the steps of the synagogue a block from Tenth). Tom was a fixture on that block. People knew him to be non-threatening, and so greeted him. Some residents even paid him to walk their dogs. Thus, Bess was familiar with Tom. One day, instead of saying hello and passing by, she stopped and asked if he would like to share a sandwich. She sat on "his steps." They ate together and she asked if he was aware of Tenth's homeless outreach and their Sunday Bible study and dinner. According to Bess, Tom wasn't ready to go to church. But, on an extremely cold and wet day the next winter, he decided he needed to get out of the cold and get a hot meal. The relationships that he established there would last a lifetime and bring him to new life.

When Tom was sixteen, he came to Philadelphia (where his grandmother lived) to look for his father who had left. He said that his mother was very sick, in and out of nursing homes and "was unable to help us." Tom says, "I needed guidance bad, I needed something." When Tom got to Philadelphia, he was told by his grandmother that his father had already left for Tennessee. He was "saddened," he stated. Not wanting to return to Paterson, he stayed in Philadelphia. Tom states that his grandmother was a born-again Christian but, about himself he says, "I was not saved—nor was I ready to be." He would visit his grandmother, but not stay with her. "I was homeless but did not know it. I was roamin' the streets, adventuring again, feeling no pain."

Soon Tom found a job, an apartment, a girlfriend and a car. "I thought I had it made and more. Then I lost it all. One big ride downhill. With a strong drug and alcohol addiction I finally wound up strung out, homeless and helpless."

During his years living on the street Tom shared bottles, butts, crack pipes and needles. He shared the fact that three people who used the same heroin needle as he did became HIV positive and died. One of them was his sister.

Over the years, Tom was in and out of recovery. After a series of relapses, Tom had fallen back into his addiction big time. He was back to sleeping "his steps" and looked horrible. He came to see me one very hot August day. I had seen him the day before wearing a clean white tee shirt and white jeans. It had rained the night before and the temperature was in the nineties. When he came in my office, he was filthy and sweaty, smelly and crying. He said he was sick and tired of being sick and tired and was ready to let God work not only on his addiction, but on his life. He surrendered.

Tom has now been clean and sober for over ten years. He is reconciled and reunited with his wife and daughters. They are all believers in Jesus Christ. Tom is employed and recently purchased a home.

Working with addicts

When you minister to addicts, homeless or not, you will need to be available to them and you will suffer because of them. But, remember, you are not responsible for their recovery. Loving addicted persons means that you hold them accountable for their actions.

Most people who display addictive behavior deny it and blameshift. Their behavior is manipulative, people-pleasing and tyrannical. In my many years working with addicted men and women, I believe I have heard every lie, every story and every derivative thereof. Dope fiends, as one recovering addict described himself, and other abusers, are controlled by their addictions. Their drugs of choice become idols which the addict "worships"—whether alcohol, crack, cocaine, heroin, ice or other mind-altering chemicals. Each man, woman or child addict shows overall allegiance to whatever drug-god has control over them. Because of this, addicts will speak and act in manipulative ways to get what they want when they want it. They will also speak and act in manipulative ways to avoid the consequences of their actions. They will usually speak and act in pleasing ways to avoid conflict, but their goal is still to manipulate people into giving them what they want (see chapter 8, "Setting Limits in Ministry").

It is important to understand the above behavior and know how to protect yourself and your church. Designate a "point person" to provide consistent counsel to the addict or addicts. Many times addicts will turn to others for "help" after being denied what they want (perhaps money). Hearing something like "No, I can't do that," the addict will promptly try to exploit someone else he or she feels is naïve and can be manipulated. So it is vital that the point person communicate what he told the addict to others who are involved. When addicts understand that "No" means "No," they usually leave and do not come back.

But suppose this person does come back, seems repentant and joins your church. What do you do? And how do you help a member who is known to be addicted to alcohol or other drugs? It is also vital to protect the church in these cases. Consistency is important, as above, but more crucial because of the constant effect the addict has on family, deacons, elders and staff. Here, an overall plan should be developed to provide real help for the addict's recovery. Help for the family is usually necessary, too. Almost everyone is affected by the addict's destructive behavior. Remember, ministry to addicted persons is a cooperative effort. Don't work harder than the one in need or you will develop a dependent relationship. When seeking to help addicts, church leaders need to know or discover three levels of resources. Firstly, who in the church can help? Who knows about addictions? Who are the social workers, counselors, health-care workers, police, etc.? And who can network or help navigate the drug-treatment system?

Secondly, what resources do other churches have or use? Thirdly, what resources are available in the community? Specifically, what credible and successful Christ-centered programs are accessible to the need at hand? If you have a working knowledge of these three, then there is no need to "reinvent the wheel" and struggle to find appropriate help.

It is easy for you, your pastor or other leaders to want to do all the work. Setting limits, delegating to others and using available resources will strengthen the body and protect you all from burnout as well. Working with an addicted person affects us all personally. Many years ago, I could be manipulated easily. My need for personal approval—from anyone—was great. So I would give an addict what he wanted. I was afraid to say "No" to actual strangers for fear they would not like me. Don't let that happen to you. Provide tough love in situations that call for it. It doesn't matters whether addicts like you. What matters is that you tell them the truth. If they do not like the truth, that is their problem. Your goal is to please God, not people.

If addicts really want help they will respect the truth. Those who want to recover from their addiction will come back. Telling the truth with Christian love will set a good foundation for focusing on the God of truth who alone can provide complete recovery from addicted behavior. God is the one who is ultimately in control of the recovery time. He is in control of the transformation of each one who comes to him for help. This, of course, does not minimize the pain and suffering you, your leaders, families and church endure. What this does is help you set limits on what your and others' responsibilities are, help you rely on the expertise that is available in your church and community and help you trust God for all things.

Working with addicts means going beyond your comfort zone. Serving them takes you into situations of pain and suffering, and that usually means bearing their burdens. Many years ago, I dined with several addicts. Over the course of the meal, they answered my questions about how they felt about themselves. One described himself as "a loser," and another, "a no-good, rotten bastard." However they phrased it, each shared a negative self-image. They all felt unworthy. As I heard their words, I felt the weight of their burdens. And it brought me to the truth. Without Jesus they are losers. They are no good. They are rotten. And they are illegitimate. But, with Jesus they can become victorious, adopted children, and heirs of a great salvation inheritance to the glory of God. This is why you serve.

5

Those Who Serve and Why They Do

Every person in the church can serve. No one is "useless." Everyone has a gift to give. Seniors can serve and be models and mentors for others. I encourage those who are no longer employed to "retire to serve." Empty nesters who suddenly have no children in the home and can serve should serve. Young marrieds, after an appropriate time to themselves, should take advantage of opportunities to serve together. Single men and women have time to share for service. Teens should be encouraged to serve and youth groups should be involved in helping others together. Children too can serve—like Peter.

Ten-year-old Peter wanted to be a table host at a dinner with our homeless neighbors. So, he was excited about speaking with me about the opportunity. I too was excited and said the ministry would welcome his service . . . if his parents were with him. You should have seen his dejected expression when he heard that. "They'd never sit with the homeless," he said. "But," I explained, "there are other ways you and your family can serve together. And none are more or less important than the others: Setting up tables, putting out utensils, napkins and tracts, food prep. All are needed." When he heard those words, he smiled. "They'll help with that," he said. The following dinner he was there. His parents were there too. We want to utilize the gifts, time and talents of the whole body of Christ at Tenth (and elsewhere) in ministry to those who are in need.

One of our goals in the ACTS Ministries is to provide Tenth Church members with unique opportunities that will utilize the full diversity of their talents and gifts, and, at the same time, place them in situations where personal relationships with others is possible. This is in accordance with Tenth's mandate for service:

> The Lord Jesus Christ set the pattern for Christian service when he washed the disciples' feet on the eve of his crucifixion. In following this pattern, Tenth Presbyterian Church desires to serve the community in which God has placed it by a variety of service ministries.[24]

Most churches have similar mandates and those in leadership should create similar goals for their mercy ministries. If you have a vision for your church, make it known. Help others see what you see. Won't you respond by integrating mercy ministry in the structure of your church like these below?

New City Fellowship, St. Louis: In response to the biblical mandate to meet human needs (Matt. 25:34–40, James 1:27) and in support of the NCF Pastors and Elders (Acts 6:1–6), the Deacons are to lead the congregation in demonstrating biblical stewardship and acts of mercy, justice and compassion to the family of believers (Gal. 6:9–10), strangers and prisoners (Heb. 13:1–3), immigrants and refugees (Deut. 10:18–19), enemies (Luke 6:27–36) and anyone in need (Luke 10:25–27).

Briarwood PCA, Birmingham: God has called us to put love into action by loving our neighbors as ourselves. Briarwood answers this call, in part, through the Mercy Ministry. Overseen by the Diaconate, the Mercy Ministry is responsible for distributing mercy funds, responding to needs of members in the community and reaching out through mercy programs to seek the lost.

Redeemer PCA, New York: As Christ came to this world to serve rather than to be served, we desire for those in our congregations to regularly serve both in our Sunday ministries and through Hope for New York to help the poor and marginalized of New York City.

As you are able and as you are led by the Lord, encourage your church to serve others in mercy ministry.

An infrastructure for service

To encourage Tenth's members to serve in our ministry to homeless persons, I enlisted the help of the leaders of Tenth's six geographic parishes. I contacted each parish elder, met with each parish council, defined the problem and desire to involve the parish, defined how leaders can effectively mobilize members for effective ministry and provided training.

Parish Boundaries

Parish One consists of Center City and South Philadelphia. At the beginning of 2013 the parish had 378 members, including twelve officers. Parish Two includes Philadelphia north of Girard Avenue, plus Bucks and Montgomery Counties. It had 395 members, including twelve officers.

Parish Three includes Philadelphia west of the Schuylkill River, Southwest Philadelphia and several small towns. It had 225 members, including five officers. Parish Four extends to the west beyond Philadelphia, generally between West Chester Pike and the Schuylkill River, plus West Chester. It had 196 members, including seven officers. Parish Five includes portions of Delaware and Chester Counties and the state of Delaware. It had 88 members, including five officers. Parish Six represents all members residing in mid- to South Jersey, from Princeton to Atlantic County, with the majority across the Delaware River from Philadelphia. It had 383 members, including twelve officers.

Contacting the Elders

I spoke individually with each of the parish elders. This was the initial conversation regarding parish participation. Next, I wrote each of the elders. I explained the opportunities for service and requested a meeting with their parish leaders (elders, deacons, small group facilitators) to propose their help in organizing a parish-sponsored ministry. By working in Community Dinners or Fellowship Bible Study, members of each parish could train together and then fellowship, pray and minister together. In addition, it would allow them occasions to meet members they did not know and, also, work with those who are their friends or acquaintances.

When I discussed with the leaders ACTS need for more volunteers, their common concern was that they already had enough on their plates. I spoke to these fears by saying that it is not the leader's job to do all the work, but it is his or her job to see that ministry occurs through others. I explained that if they merely encouraged participation, I would provide the ministry opportunities and the training. When I shared this, the leaders felt better about their task.

The leaders were also concerned about how their members would perceive volunteering with Community Dinners. One leader said, "People are fearful of the homeless." "Many don't have time," said another, "They have too many priorities already." I addressed this matter of fear, time and priorities by answering a question I often hear, "What can one person do?" My answer to those who ask the question is that one person can do his or her best, no matter how large or small. If one man's best is to volunteer one hour a week, it gives honor to God. If one woman's best is one hour a month, it glorifies God. Practically everyone can give a little, and it all adds up to a lot. Ministry can be made convenient, specific and measurable so everyone can be involved, and, as a body working together, they can make a big difference. Training and dialogue about homeless people helped resolve most fears. Speaking with experienced volunteers calmed the rest.

Every member is a minister

I listed and discussed with the parish leaders specific, measurable ways members can serve. Adults and teenagers can serve by (1) hosting a table and providing Christian hospitality to someone who is not often treated with love and/or kindness, (2) graciously serving food and drink to the ten to fifteen tables of six guests and two hosts, (3) preparing food and cleaning up, (4) providing security by monitoring various doorways during the dinner, (5) donating monetary gifts to sustain this faith ministry, (6) providing music and song for our special worship services, (7) greeting our guests and (8) bringing the gospel message.

I discussed how families with children can participate and work together too. Immediately after worship, parents can set up tables and chairs while their children place eating utensils, napkins, cups and tracts on the tables. There are also opportunities for families to work together in the kitchen. And, for those who will, families can sit together with our guests, some of whom bring their own children. This is a unique learning opportunity for the whole family. Overall, everyone is needed. Everyone can help.

In addition to working directly with the parishes, a variety of other methods were used to promote involvement among church members. I met with various small group Bible studies. Pulpit and bulletin announcements shared prayer concerns, ministry and training opportunities, and people were encouraged to sign up for ministry involvement using pew cards.

The parish response

One parish set the pace. Its elder mobilized his parish to sponsor the entire dinner. Members gave donations, purchased the food, helped cook and acted as table hosts. Families set up and cleaned up, prepared food and served the meal. Their elder set a valuable precedent by showing examples of servant-leadership. He communicated the needs, delegated authority, followed up to ensure work was accomplished and then showed up to host a table. The work of this parish helped establish a model for others parishes and groups to follow.

Goals achieved

The parish elders "signed on" to participate twice a year, once every six months. In the first year, the number of volunteer workers increased. All told, there was an increase of fifty-eight members to the large number who already participated. This did not include all the people who worked behind the scenes to coordinate and organize the parish's involvement. Since then members have eagerly shown up to help during their parish's turn. Many now participate regularly and mercy has become more and more a fabric of the Tenth life.

What I learned

I said at the beginning of this chapter that everyone can serve. No one is useless. Imagine how surprised I was to see who volunteered. Sure, there were your able-bodied men, women and teens. But, there were also differently-abled folks. These included a sight-impaired member and her service dog. A woman serving from her wheelchair wanted to share the meal with our guests. A husband and wife with their special needs children volunteered. Also, an adult member who is developmentally challenged served and showed us he is quite an evangelist.

Because the elders and other leaders grasped my idea, they were able to transfer that to parish members, who are now volunteers. It was easier than I had imagined and is easily reproducible elsewhere. You can mobilize your church too, working with small groups like Bible studies or larger groups such as a geographic parish. I encourage you to communicate the needs around you and opportunities to meet those needs. Model the servant character of Christ and show that everyone can serve. God will stir up members' hearts and bring the volunteers to serve.

Sharing our hearts

In addition to the mobilization mentioned above, I facilitated a focus group with twelve of my volunteers.[25] I was interested in what motivated them. Why did they serve? Take note of the reasons they've expressed. Jot down ideas that will help you in your own church context.

Some indicated they acted as a response to Scripture. "The Bible tells us to love God and our neighbors. My involvement is a response to grace." Another commented, "If you are in the Word of God, how can you not listen and consider the needs of others?" For them, it was the Word that drew them to serve. When you ask people to pray about ministry opportunities, they too will to listen to the Word of God as they consider the needs of others.

Relationships drew one couple. "I wanted to be involved in ministry where I can work with my spouse. I believe that relationships are important." Reflecting on the ways your members would like to serve will point you to a variety of opportunity options.

Some shared a desire to share their faith. "I enjoy speaking about the Word—it's part of a lifestyle for me, seeing God at work. There's hope for now and for all eternity." Then there was the importance of encouragement. "Ministry of encouragement is important. I enjoy showing God's love. It's hospitality in Jesus' name. And, God can use everybody in the church—not just adults—kids too." You have many members with the gifts of evangelism and encouragement. Think of ways for them to practice those gifts.

Serving produces heart change

When I asked how ministry had changed them, there were several comments about the process of spiritual growth. One respondent answered, "I've matured through this ministry. I'm compelled to walk my talk before others." Another spoke about the depth of growth. "I have matured in prayer and Bible study. I now take opportunities to grow deeper and be more prepared. I'm motivated and overjoyed." And another, "I've become more compassionate. I now see others as Christ sees them." As people serve, they grow. Think of the small steps you can take to make this happen. What is your ministry passion?

Several task force members spoke of role models and books they had read. One mentioned *They Dare to Love the Ghetto* by Keith Phillips. Another, after reading *Christ + City* by Jon Dennis said, "He talks about Christians relocating in the city and persevering with God's help." Another said, "I read a book by John Perkins [founder of Christian Community Development Association]. That book and prayer got me involved." Who are your ministry role models? What books can you recommend to motivate others?

One respondent spoke about a homeless guest. "I get motivated by watching Al's growth. Seeing his transformation from being homeless and addicted reminds me of the verse from the prophet Joel, something about restoring the years that the locusts have eaten (see Joel 2:25)." Another found encouragement from those they shared ministry with. "My coworkers in ministry are encouraging role models. I think a proverb says he who walks with a wise man is wise (see Prov. 13:20)." One member stated that one of her parents had turned her on to service. "My mother showed me. Her actions impressed me—she used to bring coats to people who had no coats. I started serving as a tutor mentoring at-risk children and then cooking for our Community Dinners for the homeless."

The consensus of the task force was that Christianity not practiced in serving others is just a self-centered religion. They shared from Matthew 25:35–36 that ministry to the poor and needy is an expression of how much we love God. You can demonstrate this same attitude in your church.

Remember, every member is a minister. Every member has the capacity to serve in some way. Listen to one of the respondents. "As a disabled person I have often been excluded from helping and seen as a burden. I found it difficult to become involved as a volunteer in other churches. In fact, this was a contributing factor, years ago, to my loss of faith. Every church I tried excluded me from volunteering. But at Tenth, it's wonderful to be able to share what I have with others. It's wonderful to be needed."

6

Unwrapping the Graveclothes

Ministries of mercy and compassion require that people work closely with those who are hurting and vulnerable. On many occasions, we will find ourselves unwrapping the graveclothes of the walking dead.

Martha probably knew what they all would experience when Jesus commanded in John 11:39 that the stone in front of Lazarus' grave be removed. The smell of death is unmistakable. And she objected, saying, "Lord, by this time there will be a stench" (NASB). Jesus then prayed and called forth Lazarus from the grave, loud enough that those nearby would hear. Lazarus was wrapped in graveclothes—strips of white linen cloth used to wrap a dead body with and with spices to cover its strong odor of decay. Verse 44 tells us: "The man who had died came out, his hands and feet bound with linen strips, and his face wrapped with a cloth." Jesus said to those nearby, "Unbind him, and let him go." Thus the scene that the Gospel of John describes, and what everyone within hearing distance witnessed, was Jesus calling to a dead man. And Lazarus came forth alive and standing, still bound hand and foot with graveclothes. What Jesus did next was call His followers to action, "Unbind him, and let him go," that is, loose him, and free him from his bonds.

As the vessels God uses to facilitate His work, we also must be ready to unravel, loose and free from bondage those He has called us to.

At a Mercy Ministry Conference for the Presbyterian Church in America organization, Dr. Diane Langberg, a Christian psychiatrist who treats victims of traumatic stress and abuse, shared what she saw while encouraging counselors who worked with first responders at ground zero in New York. Many of us can clearly remember what happened on September 11, 2001 when four planes were hijacked and crashed into the World Trade Center in New York City, the Pentagon in Washington, DC and a field in Schwenksville, PA . How can we ever forget its horror? The rescuers were in a place of utter ruin—sifting through the rubble looking for people. Langberg describes the horror: "There was so much: Workers looking for those who might still be alive . . . breathing the stench of death while digging in the tombs. The rescuers overwhelmed with the enormity of suffering and trauma . . . experiencing the unthinkable . . . needing to share with someone but dreading it, remaining silent in the unbearable suffering. . . . Seeing again and again what should not be endured. Wanting to remove its memory to bury it in a different kind of tomb."[26]

Langberg compared the rescue efforts during 9/11 to Christians who also "work in the tombs"—those people called by God to bring people to life from fear, disease, despair and trauma. But, she said, this kind of ministry can only happen when our own lives are transformed through the life of Christ and the power of His resurrection. If we are going to attempt to minister in the tombs, she said, we must first be made into instruments God can use in this divine mission. We are ordinary people put to work by the Almighty God and given extraordinary responsibility to dispense resurrection-life, bringing God's character to places where nothing resembles him. Ordinary people taking His light and life into dark, ugly places.[27]

We cannot be afraid to speak about the dark and ugly. We must do so in order to know where to shine Christ's light and show His beauty. We need to shine His light on sex trafficking, murders, urban and suburban evils, the rape and battering of women and children and the hidden physical abuse that occurs in marriages. There is suffering everywhere. God's creation is ruined by suffering, despair, brokenness and darkness.

Following Jesus as His servants

Yet, there is no quick fix in those ruins. The true rescue is God's long-term work—and no evil, no suffering, is outside Christ's redemptive capability. Redemption is an invitation for us to follow Jesus and walk among people in the darkness of their utter ruin. Redemption leads us to say, as Isaiah, "Here I am! Send me" (Isa. 6:8). And, "Here we are, cleansed and touched by God, bearing the power of His resurrection, send us to the tombs." Redeemed, we are led out of our own tombs to follow Jesus in pouring ourselves out on behalf of others.

Following Jesus means that we prayerfully walk into places of poverty, captivity, darkness and evil. Caring for the traumatized, we are called into partnership with Christ. We are called to obediently follow a Savior who was, Himself, traumatized for our sake (53:4–5). And the strength to do so can only be gathered through a relationship with Christ. We may sit across from a victimized friend or an abused wife or another victim of violence. We may be called to help with a national disaster recovery. Unless we are filled again and again with the Living Bread we will be of little use.

As a social worker in my early career, I attempted to do it on my own. What I discovered was if we try to raise the walking dead on our own, they remain the walking dead. We cannot persevere in the stench, darkness and evil every day without immersing ourselves in worship and prayer. To work among the dead we need the resurrection of Christ in us— in the dark and dead places in us. We must bow to the work of God in our lives. Working in the tombs is the Father's resurrection work.

Years ago I conducted a survey with a group who attend Fellowship Bible Study. Over time I noticed that when we ended with the Lord's Prayer many remained silent. Thus, my survey— a follow-up consisting of only one question: "Why can't you say *Our Father*?"

What I discovered was that seven out of ten of these men and women had been raped or sexually abused as children by a father, uncle, older brother, teacher or pastor—some male authority figure. This prevented them from praying "Our Father" or going to our heavenly Father for help at any time. Because of their distorted image of God, they cringed when they thought of God as Father. All they could think of was the one who abused them and crushed their spirit. It took years working with this particular group, peeling back the layers of pain and suffering, for them to gradually feel comfortable saying "Our Father, who art in heaven. . . ." They all wanted to live in a healthy relationship with Christ, but were burdened with layers and layers of abusive memories and the darkness of their own tombs. It took me and others a long period of time to remove the graveclothes in which they were wrapped. Slowly and carefully we unwrapped the cloths that kept them trapped in death's tomb. Slowly and carefully we brought God's light and life to shine through.

People and choices: Light in the darkness

There was no light shining through Mary. No, Mary was difficult—a crack addict who we ministered to for over ten years. During this time, she lived on the street, sold her body for sex and drugs and had multiple pregnancies in the process. The result of her lifestyle was that she cared for none of her children— all were aborted or taken by Child Protective Services. She attended our Sunday Bible studies because there was always a meal and a change of clothing, but she regularly refused our help with her addiction, lifestyle and need for salvation. She received the food and clothing and kindness, but ignored her greater needs. If anyone was a master manipulator, it was Mary. Many times during the week, she would come into the church lobby demanding help and on two or three occasions either soiled herself or menstruated on the furniture to ensure we would give her what she wanted—just to get her to leave. After years of this we told Mary we would not help her anymore and that she was no longer welcome at Tenth. After she left, I recall how I went to my office, locked the door, sat down and wept. I sobbed tears of sorrow over her condition and our inability to unbind her and free her from her deathly existence. And I prayed.

Two years later, one of our volunteer staff spoke with Mary on the street. She was clean and sober and a new creature in Christ. God had brought her so low in her darkness that she hit bottom harder than she ever had before. As a result she cried out to Him for help and entered a Christian recovery program where she surrendered her life to Jesus. Her heart was no longer hardened toward God.

*   *   *

Frank was an inveterate criminal whose heart was hardened toward God. When we first met him in prison, he was awaiting his sentencing. To avoid some of his cellblock's violence and monotony, he attended our Bible study. He attended the first week, then a month, then two. He never paid much attention and never read his Bible. Then, unexpectedly, he was missing from the study. One week, two, then a month, forty-five days. When he returned something was different, and he shared the story of being put in solitary for an offense (he didn't share what it was). Allowed to have his New Testament but angry at God, he did not open the Bible for two weeks. But, then, desperate, he turned to Ephesians, the book used in our Bible study. He read it once, then again and again, and was hungry for more. He continued reading the other Epistles and Gospels, and on day twenty-nine, in the darkness of his cell, he fell on his knees and surrendered his life to the one who was now his Savior. When he returned to the Bible study everyone was astounded by the change they saw.

The following week, Frank went to court filled with a new confidence, that is, until he received an unexpected twenty-seven year sentence and was slated for transportation to another facility soon after. Angry, he asked God, "Why? Why are doing this to me?"

God answered a month later when in the new facility his new cellmate was talking about suicide. Frank forgot about himself and shared his new found hope of Christ with the cellmate—and Frank himself was renewed. In God's providence, he proclaimed that he was now an "inside minister" and would serve the Lord in this new mission field for as long as he was doing time.

God had used our Bible study to bring Frank from darkness to light. And in that lonely cell, the God of Life confronted the power of death, calling Frank out of his tomb. Frank's story is about God using His people to bring "the new life of resurrection peace."

Peace beyond understanding

Peace was not what the woman at the well had in John 4. You know the story. She went at noon to get water from a well outside her village. Jesus came and asked her to give Him a drink. Then they had a conversation about life and lifestyles.

Here is the scenario: She was a woman, obviously, and it was culturally wrong for a woman to meet alone with a man who was not her husband. Ethnically, she was a Samaritan, and Jews and Samaritans had a long-seated hatred toward one another, so whenever possible, Jews avoided going through Samaria. Jesus was also a rabbi. The law said He would become ceremonially unclean by being with any Samaritan. The law even hinted that if a Samaritan's shadow touched a Jew, he would be unclean for seven days.

So, she comes to the well, the Bible says, at the sixth hour— twelve o'clock. Why at noon and not earlier when it was cooler? Why not use the well in her village? The reason is she was an outcast, stigmatized by her community, so she went for water at the hottest time of the day, assuring herself that she would be alone and no one would harass her. And she didn't go to the local well, but one a distance away, to be free from those who would gossip, criticize and judge her. But, just when she thought she was safe, Jesus comes to the well.

How did Jesus treat her? Differently. While He knew her sinful lifestyle, He focused on the tomb she had dug for herself, and He took the time to show kindness and concern rather than judgment. And her response to His graciousness? Her response was to receive living water from His well and to then run to tell her village of the Messiah's coming.

Sharing the hope found in Christ

Bobby was very much like the woman at the well. She knew what it was like to be stigmatized. Bobby was HIV positive and sought the help of an agency for people with AIDS. At the same time, she sought spiritual support and began attending Fellowship Bible study. Sometime later, she became a believer—even as her illness took its toll. After a two-year battle with AIDS, Bobby died. Several Bible study members and I attended her memorial service which was led by a leader in her AIDS support group. The service was dark. It offered no light or hope, and there was no mention of Bobby's faith in Christ. This concerned me, so, following the service I introduced myself to the agency's director—explaining our relationship with Bobby, how she studied the Bible with us—and asked him if we could conduct a Bible study at his agency. He said he could not make the decision alone—it was something the staff and community members would have to agree upon together. He arranged a meeting the following week.

Forty people attended the meeting, representing members of the GLBT community—gays, lesbians, bisexuals and transvestites—plus intravenous drug users, agency staff and several members of Tenth. When it was my turn to speak, I explained our relationship with Bobby, how Bobby had become a believer, how she had profound joy in her new life in Christ and the hope of eternal life. I said that our desire (and hoped-for outcome of this meeting) was to teach the Bible to those who sought help through their agency and to establish relationships with those who attended the study. Some at this meeting recalled positively how Bobby shared her testimony of how God had freed her from sin's dark tomb. There were many others, however, who responded only in anger saying, "Are you that gay-bashing church?" And asking, "Will you try to change us? Are you going to try to make us Presbyterian? What about gays? Are you going to forbid homosexuals from attending? And cross-dressers . . . certainly you won't allow transvestites to attend?"

To these questions and others, I repeated the reasons already stated for the Bible study: we wanted to share the hope in Christ and new life that Bobby found in the Bible, and we wanted to develop relationships with those who would attend the new study. We said that we could not change anyone's behavior— only God could. We said we were not teaching our opinions but only the Word of God found in the Bible. We said everyone is welcome to attend and that the study, which would be held in this very room, would not be a platform for "gay bashing." We would begin with the Gospel of John, chapter one verse one, and progress from there. And, if the text mentioned the sin of murder, we'd discuss it—the same with idolatry, alcoholism, adultery, sexual sins and others. We referred again and again to our relationship with Bobby and the new hope that she had as a person dealing with AIDS. After more haranguing and much discussion, one person stood up, looked around the room, threw his hands in the air and said, "Well, what the hell. Why not? We need all the help we can get!" I looked around the room and saw each person nodding his or her head in agreement. As a result, a weekly Bible study was established. The first and second weeks were met with protests by the gay activist group *Act Up*, but that was the only interruption to a growing and then well-attended Bible study. Some from this group began attending Fellowship Bible Study and Tenth worship, and six months later, we were asked to conduct a worship service there. God had used Bobby to bring hope to a group of people battling for their lives and seeking peace with God.

Another kind of resurrection

Kay certainly needed the peace Christ gives us all. She was happily married to a faithful husband—or so she thought. Her husband, a seminary student, was involved in a variety of ministries and was out of the home at least two evenings a week. So it was never a surprise that his schedule took him away. What did surprise her one day was finding a pack of condoms between the seat cushions of their car. This led Kay to confront her husband with what she found, which led to other painful details. He was indeed unfaithful—not once, but many times, as his escapades over the last two years took him to prostitutes again and again. Her life was now in chaos. She worried that her marriage had ended and feared that her husband might be carrying a sexually transmitted disease and had infected her. The weight of all this was too much for her and she described the experience as "a truckload of bricks falling on me." She was crushed and felt dead.

My wife and I reached out to Kay and her children. We offered her the hospitality of our home and took time to listen and pray with her. She also found support among those in our divorce recovery ministry. They knew what she was experiencing and understood her. Gradually God began a healing process, enough that Kay started reaching out to other abused spouses with the help and comfort that she'd received. Once again, it took the right people and the right amount of time for them to unwrap her graveclothes and help Kay in this grievous situation.

We must help

Perhaps you know someone who is bearing the weight of the world, grieving a loss or living in the tombs due to some abuse or trauma. What hurting person has God placed you near? Who is God calling you to come alongside? What role is He calling you to play in another person's life?

We are called to help those who are hurting and to "unwrap the graveclothes" of those grieving and left for dead, broken or weak, vulnerable and feeling unwanted. When Jesus said, "Unwrap the graveclothes," He pretty much said, "Help Me help the Lazaruses of this world." Some will want to say, "I can't. That stone is too heavy to roll away!" or "Unwrapping the dead is too difficult!" Nevertheless, we are called to the task. Jesus raises the dead, but He uses us to unwrap the graveclothes.

"Jesus calls us o'er the tumult"[28] to dispense God's mercy and compassion to others and to take His love and beauty into ugly places. We are called to work in the tombs among the "dead" who are still alive. In essence, as we walk among the poor, broken, despairing and those who mourn, we must walk as Jesus walked. Like Jesus in Luke 4:18, we must read Isaiah 61:1 as if the verse were speaking about us. "The Spirit of the Lord is upon us, because he has anointed us to proclaim good news to the poor. He has sent us to proclaim liberty to the captives and recovering of sight to the blind, to set at liberty those who are oppressed." We must walk in the prisons, the dark places, even the tombs, where people reside. We, like the rescuers at the World Trade Center, are first responders in the lives of those who suffer.

As "first responders" we minister to others in their distress. We serve in the distressed places of this world showing the love and beauty of Christ. We bring His goodness to places of need, trauma and suffering in accordance with the depth of our worship and prayer.

Without a deep and abiding walk with Christ, we will surely lose heart or even burn out. Remember, descending into the tombs is resurrection work. It is an invitation to Calvary for us as children to rely on the help of our Father.

I love Rev. Mo Leverett's illustration about the father-love. Founder of Desire Street Ministries in New Orleans, Mo walked among those who suffered, living with and helping residents in one of the poorest sections of New Orleans. He tells the story of how, as a father, he has the help of his children.

> In the early days, our family would sometimes go on trips, and periodically we would have to stop and get gas. My children loved to get out of the car and help me pump the gas. As a matter of fact, they loved to do anything I did. On this particular occasion they were fighting over who got to help. And so I intervened and said, "It's okay, you can all help." And so all my kids come bouncing out of the car. I told Lindsey, my oldest, "Lindsey, you put your hands on top of your dad's hands," because Lindsey was not strong enough to hold the handle. And I said, "Lacy, you put your hand on top of your sister's hand." Then to Maggie, I said, "You hold your daddy's leg." If you had seen us, you would have been at the very least amused.
>
> I invited them into my work. Why? Because my children found joy being with their father in his work. The reason we carry out God's mercy is not so much to fill some requirement. It's about being with our Father—sharing His heart, His mission, and His work.[29]

In the lives of those suffering, Christ uses us to roll stones away and unbind the dead. Christ calls and says to us, "Help me help this person. Help me help that person." We aren't needed, but our Father wants us to participate with Him in His resurrection work.

As we decide to participate in ministry, we will discover that God the Father has preceded us and is with us. We will see, as Leverett, above, that we are just putting our hands on His hands, our arms around His leg, watching Him do what only He can do.

7

You Don't Have to Reinvent the Wheel

There are many opportunities that allow Christians to serve in our churches, neighborhoods and communities. Explore the ministry landscape, and you can see what other churches and religious organizations are offering. You can also discover what is available in government and private social services. The information gathered will present you with a sense of what is missing. Imagine asking the question, "How can our church offer a Christ-centered alternative to what the world is providing?" If you do ask such a question, you will need knowledge of what to do (or not to do) next. I'd like to share some ideas, my own how-to guide, for ministry development.

Identifying the gaps

What are the opportunities for your ministry? There seems to be no end to opportunities for serving others. There are many needy groups: alcoholics, drug addicts, homeless, illiterate, mentally disabled, migrant workers, unemployed, working poor; elderly, widows; single parent, divorced, unwed mothers;

disadvantaged children, abused and neglected children, juvenile delinquents, learning disabled, physically disabled; blind, deaf; chronically ill, terminally ill; prisoners, ex-offenders; refugees, immigrants, international students; and disaster victims.

As I said, there are many.

Tenth has ministered to prison inmates and their children, nursing home residents, divorced and separated men and women, single parents, homeless and addicted men and women, incarcerated men and women, elementary and high school students, college students, international students, women seeking abortions, people with AIDS and victims of sexual abuse. I will describe our experience in establishing four ministries: in a prison, juvenile detention facility, public school and public library.

It may be the desire of church leaders to start a ministry because it is important to "get going." Many invest themselves in being busy for the sake of being busy. However, in order to avoid the tyranny of the urgent, it is important that leaders consider five principles: planning ahead wisely, learning from others, learning from the past, anticipating the future and counting the costs. These principles will guide leaders and help prevent them from having to go back to the drawing board again and again. It will also help them avoid problems, frustrations, failure and burnout. Leaders who follow these principles will also avoid having to "reinvent the wheel." Again, the goal of the "starting-a-ministry process" is not to keep people busy. The goal of developing new ministries is to glorify God and benefit those we seek to serve.

Counting the costs

As you venture into ministry development, make sure that your proposed ministry actually meets a genuine need. Early in the ministry's history, an ACTS leader wanted to develop a ministry for recording books on tape for the nursing home residents we served. It was a wonderful idea. But, as we found out later, there was no need. For two years, volunteers worked to record the tapes. We produced their labels. We arranged to get tape players from the Library for the Blind. Volunteers gave time, effort and love preparing the tapes for use, but we found in the end that no one wanted them. The nursing home residents said they were satisfied with the local library's recorded book service and could even obtain some of the religious books we produced. Our volunteers were discouraged and I was disappointed— disappointed with the result. Yet, we learned a lesson. Make sure there is a real need before you try to meet it.

As you consider starting a new ministry, think of the problems you may encounter. What obstacles could you face? Early in ACTS Ministries' development, the biggest obstacles were leaders and others opposed to our working with homeless persons. Actually, they were not antagonistic to that work. They were opposed to our ministering to homeless men and women in the church building! So, we sought to build bridges to lovingly win them over. There were individual meetings and small group meetings on the ministry itself, and there were seminars and conferences on the biblical aspect of our mercy ministry. And we prayed. As a result, people gained a new perspective as we presented facts about the ministry, who the homeless were, how we would serve, and—especially—what security measures we had in place. And the more we taught about the Bible and the poor, the more the Holy Spirit moved people's hearts.

As you venture into this process, do not neglect prayer and its power. Invite people to pray and ask God to show them the rightness of your ministry. In our experience, many not only ended their opposition, but became supporters.

Planning ahead

The planning phase of ministry development is extremely critical. Below are several items to consider. Most importantly pray. Begin with prayer. Be steadfast in prayer. Pray without ceasing. Did I say to pray? Picture the ministry. Place it before God.

As I mentioned, ask if your ministry meets a specific need. What is the need and who are its proposed recipients? Is another church or agency currently meeting this need? If so, how will yours be uniquely different? Develop a committee to thoroughly explore these issues. Include wise, experienced church leaders and those with memories of past efforts. Build bridges with different people and groups and gain ownership by the leaders.

You will need to consider finances. Do you need a guaranteed source of funds before proceeding? Is funding part of the church's budget? Is funding automatically renewable, and if so, for how long? Is funding contingent on grant applications? Who will write the grant application?

You will need a steering committee or board of directors. Will fund-raising be the domain of the board of directors or that of the ministry coordinator? If it is the ministry coordinator's responsibility, this will limit his focus on the ministry itself. Also, what type of accountability structure will you have (controlling or advisory board)? Consider the benefits of people guiding you versus people dictating to you (you may feel that way). How would you benefit from a controlling board of directors? Will the board give freedom and ownership to the ministry coordinator? Will he or she be tied to a hitching post or led by a lamppost?

You will need trained ministry staff. Make sure adequate training is available. You can do this yourself or better yet, cooperate with other churches or church groups (presbyteries, etc.). Local agencies—nursing homes, homeless shelters, hospitals, police departments, etc.—frequently have open-to-the-public training. The internet is a wealth of information with "how-to manuals." Vimeo.com has a wealth of training films (search for Tenth Presbyterian training for some of ours). Tenth.org is presently placing written, audio and video diaconal training on its site.

Remember, there are natural consequences to your actions. You want to plan wisely and be ready with the right resources to "intercept the future" when it arrives. Respect God's timetable. Be deliberate and careful (do it once and do it right). And continue to pray.

Learning from the past and anticipating the future

Every organization has a particular ministry "culture"—a specific way of doing ministry. Some church's leaders might say, "We don't do it that way here." Or "We tried that once and it didn't work." Examine your church's history of ministry accomplishments, successes and learning experiences. Speak with those who possess vibrant memories of these experiences. How would they characterize the "culture" of your church? Would you say it is open or ready for new ministries and/or new ways of doing ministry?

Do you believe change is necessary? Why would it be a good thing? Ask the question, "What will happen if we do things differently (and it works)?" How will the result benefit the church and community? What will be the short-term benefit? Long-term? Imagine what you want your church to look like in ten to twenty years.

Anticipate spiritual attack. Who are the prayer warriors who can bathe these plans in prayer? Mobilize them. Pray. Pray some more.

Put it into practice

One way to renew church ministry is to see a need and do something about it. Tenth Presbyterian Church has over 180 years of tradition. Changing a ministry paradigm is like turning an ocean liner completely around. It takes time and depends on the cooperation of many staff members. But it can happen.

Most of Tenth's outreach ministries started from the bottom up. People who had burdens for a particular people group were led to set a vision. They started City Center Academy (urban Christian high school), Alpha Pregnancy Services (alternatives to abortion), Harvest USA (homosexuality and sexual addictions), Hope (HIV/AIDS) and ACTS Ministries (diaconal/mercy).

And while there were some obstacles, including the NIMBY principle (not in my back yard, i.e., church!), for some, biblical principles superseded those attitudes and fears. It took perseverance, prayer, support, encouragement and more prayer to change attitudes and make the ministry paradigm more pliable. One of the most important lessons I have learned is we can't change other people. We must wait and pray and trust God to do the changing. And what started as programs to others (with a clear separation of us and them), became a blend of hospitality ministries with our guests and for our guests. We get involved (show up), establish relationships and offer hope. We make it welcoming and safe for our guests as many have lost the support of churches, families and friends. Establishing personal relationships helps remove the stigma and the stranger-ness which our guests have felt in most churches.

We also make it user-friendly for our members to be involved, equipping them to fearlessly come alongside others. We make ministry convenient, measurable and specific. And our ministry philosophy is that while we advocate, we don't work harder than the people coming for help. We seek to empower without creating a relationship of dependency. Here are some "start-up" stories.

School partnerships

One of the things we did at Tenth was pray about serving our local school and its students. We prayed as a group and we did prayerwalks around the school property. We then sought to develop a partnership with the public school two blocks away, which began by establishing relationships with its various administrators. We had worked on this for six months when the school principal was suddenly transferred to another school. We prayerfully waited another six months for her replacement and proceeded, once again, to develop a healthy relationship with the new principal. After months of building bridges, the principal shared that the school was chosen to be closed by the Board of Education. Following its closure months later, as we prayed about the next step and the next school, the Philadelphia Board of Education announced that it was establishing "faith partnerships" between houses of worship and neighborhood schools.

Intrigued by this, I attended a meeting with representatives of the Board of Education with rabbis, imams, priests and other ministers. The head of the new faith initiative presented a broad policy for how houses of worship could help local schools, provide materials, etc. After he finished sharing this information, I raised my hand, introduced myself, and the following exchange occurred:

Me: "You understand that we're a church and our allegiance is to the God of the Bible. We do want to establish a partnership with a local school. What can we do again?"

Rep: "You can do anything except proselytize."

Me: "I've always found that word interesting. How do you define proselytize?"

Rep: "How do you define it?"

Me: "For me, proselytizing is putting the Bible on the end of a baseball bat and beating people over the head with it. But we're not going to do that. Our hope is to go into the school, establish relationships with the principal and her staff and place people in the classroom to help the teachers—to be as helpful and cooperative as we can be. And, if anyone asks why we're doing this, we would share the reason. We are followers of Jesus Christ.

Rep: "That's okay."

Speaking with the school official later, I learned his expectation was that churches would be intolerant and belligerent—seeking to beat salvation into others. But after I defined what we were about, he said we could share our faith in the way we described. So, we went into the school and established relationships with the principal, the administrative staff and the teachers. Classroom volunteers got to know the teachers, the relationship grew stronger and we were able to share the gospel.

Serving juveniles in the criminal justice system

In 1951, The Juvenile Detention Center in Philadelphia was built not far from Tenth Church. The facility houses (incarcerates) over one hundred adolescents, ages twelve through seventeen, who have committed crimes including rape, robbery and murder. The center has a school, medical facilities, social workers, psychologists, courtrooms, religious services and special programs.

In 2005 I met with the chaplain and program director of the center. The purpose of the meeting was to discuss how Tenth members could become involved in ministry. During the course of our conversation—and thinking about issues the "residents" must face—I asked, "What are some of the problems here?" That question brought a rapid and lengthy response that focused on the issues of "stress, anger, conflict and negative attitudes." After a pause, but before I could respond, the program director continued, saying, "But that's just the staff."

"How do I reply?" I thought. Immediately the Lord prompted me to say, "What do you think about my meeting regularly for prayer with the staff?" Both the chaplain and program director said it was a great idea and asked when I could start. We continued discussing the needs of residents, and I was given the following list of needs: anger management, violence prevention, conflict resolution, dealing with feelings and health issues such as asthma, sickle-cell anemia, childhood diabetes, behavior, relationships and issues of self-worth. This was a lot to pray about.

And pray I did. These needs represented ministry opportunities. Soon Tenth members with specific expertise were entering the center, leading workshops and establishing relationships with the kids, enough that they asked our volunteer staff why they were there. Their answer? "Because the love of Jesus compels us."

Praying against the visible darkness and oppression of the facility was a paramount focus of my meetings with staff (which became a Bible study a year later). One staff member was hesitant to join because of his personal problem trusting others. "These walls have ears," he said, not wanting to join us. Yet he stood in the doorway and shared his heart with us. Others saw this as a midweek spiritual feeding. Those in the study had many questions which could be found in God's Word. The result was a small group of staff being filled with the light of Christ, bringing His light to other staff. One began reading the Bible for the first time and had been inviting colleagues to the Bible study. Another recommitted his life to Christ. Others were making their prayer requests known, even the guards. We had privacy, confidentiality and our own room to meet—until the building was torn down.

The facility was located in the middle of Philadelphia's "Museum Mile" and was scheduled to be replaced at that precious site by the internationally famed Barnes Museum. So in 2009, the detention center was demolished and temporarily relocated in a former psychiatric hospital five miles north.

Several teachers in the temporary location discovered the Bible study and it grew. That was good, but we had one problem. There was inadequate space and we had no permanent room to meet. When possible, we met in a conference room, but most of the time we met in cramped offices, hallways, storage closets and outside when the weather was agreeable. Nevertheless, we met regularly as the Spirit of God strengthened the staff for their work with the incarcerated youth.

There were questions of policy, of course. "How can I make known to the residents my renewed faith in Christ? I can't violate church-state," a health professional asked. To that I shared the importance of establishing relationships and trust, and in the context of dealing with a particular issue asking permission to share Scripture or personal hope in Christ. If the resident says "Yes" then the door is open to appropriate comments which will lead to future dialogue and greater hope. This is exactly what the workshop leaders teaching anger management and HIV/AIDS experienced.

In 2013, the Juvenile Justice Services Center finally moved to a brand new facility, and after a four month hiatus, I returned there to minister. Within five minutes of arrival, I resumed a prior conversation with one security guard and, for a brief moment, the facility felt to him less like a prison.

The federal prison

In early 1999, the Bureau of Prisons began constructing a new Federal Detention Center near Tenth. Accordingly, my prayers began to include a ministry to these future neighbors, but I had no idea what ministry at the new Federal Detention Center would look like. I made many phone calls and my contacts at the Bureau of Prisons and Prison Fellowship told me that the shape of the ministry depended on what the not-yet-hired chaplain wanted. So a small group at Tenth began praying for a Bible-believing chaplain and the relationship Tenth would have with the chaplain.

I began a dialogue with the Bureau of Prison's regional chaplain on what steps to take, people to add to the discussion and timetable for the arrival of inmates. I spoke with him monthly for updates on construction, anticipated time for completion, chaplain selection and to build a relationship. And I waited.

The prison opened in May of the following year, and prayers were answered in June with the arrival of an evangelical Southern Baptist chaplain who knew of Tenth Presbyterian Church and its long-standing ministry.

In July, August and September volunteers received twenty-four hours of volunteer training by me, Prison Fellowship and the prison staff. This ended with credentialing, criminal and child abuse database screening, fingerprinting and a tour of the facilities.

We visited the women's floor and saw the inmates looking dejected and in despair. They saw us too. Some had a look of gladness—maybe even hope. When the chaplain told them that we were church volunteers, more faces lit up and as we were leaving a couple of the women said, very sincerely, "Please come back."

We also visited a vacant unit. Each volunteer stood in a cell and prayed for the inmates who would soon occupy the space and, hopefully, would worship and attend Bible studies in this part of our neighborhood. Soon we had Tuesday night Bible studies on every floor (except the lock-down unit) and a Spanish-language worship service on Sunday. And there are more opportunities for Kingdom work. Since our ministry began, The federal prison has held the head of the Philadelphia "crime family," the mayor of Camden, nationally known rap artists and many others of notoriety. What would happen if God saved some of these?

A unique opportunity

There are an abundance of ministry opportunities in every community. Some are often unexpected and unique. Several years ago, I established a relationship with the librarian at my local library and began volunteering on my day off. He was delighted that I would offer my services and soon had me entering new books into the computer system for two to three hours every week.

One day I was asked to enter a box of best-selling books that had been donated. "Donated?" I asked myself. I wondered if they would accept books by Christian authors—books pointing to salvation in Christ. I prayed about this and asked the librarian. He said, "If the title is in the library's computer database, the donated book can be entered into the system." I checked the database and within a week I placed *Knowing God* by J.I. Packer on the library circulation shelf and then followed this with books by James Boice, R.C. Sproul and other Christian authors.

Having the title "volunteer staff" helped me establish relationships with the rest of the library employees. It also eased into a new pastoral relationship with the librarian. After many years of listening to and counseling him he finally agreed to pray with me. Months later he came to saving faith in Jesus Christ.

Recently my librarian friend discussed the city's budget crisis with me and mentioned the possibility of the library closing some branches. He said he needed prayer and asked if I would pray for him and his staff, which I did. I then asked if he would like me to lead the staff in prayer every week. His answer was an immediate "Yes" and so began a weekly devotional and a time of prayer an hour before opening time.

The library staff saw themselves as a Christian presence—a lighthouse in the neighborhood. They even prayed that God's light might be seen in them. This was seen by the patrons who noticed a difference in this community resource. One commented to an assistant librarian, "There is something different and special here that is missing in other branches." The librarian replied, "That's because Christ is in us."

You can be a Christian presence in your own neighborhood. You too can volunteer, establish relationships and offer hope. Perhaps even at your local library. There is no limit to the good you can accomplish.

8

Setting Limits in Ministry

Those who work in mercy and diaconal ministry need safe boundaries. This is a priority. The alternative of having few or no boundaries is discouragement, spiritual fatigue and burnout. We must learn how to fulfill our needs on a daily basis through a healthy balance of giving to others while also receiving affirmation and support from others and from God. People who are involved in mercy ministry make mistakes and learn from those mistakes. Personally, I've made some blunders. Early in my career I saw myself as a rescuer; I succumbed to the tyranny of the urgent and I had no safe boundaries to protect myself.

If we want to serve wisely, then we must learn to understand and respect our limitations. In order to love ourselves, we must set up reasonable boundaries. Our Lord tells us to do our best and to serve in a way that is pleasing to Him (see 1 Cor. 10:31) and that means being realistic and having common sense.

Learning from our mistakes

At the age of twenty-four, my first year as a deacon, I thought I knew what I was doing. However, I could be easily manipulated and sometimes I provided assistance out of feelings of guilt. Many times I did not establish proper limits. The truth was I did not know what I was doing. I am reminded of an incident that now seems absurd, yet it happened. I was our church's benevolence treasurer. One night, I received a telephone request from a stranger who said he needed help in paying his rent. The caller told me he was referred by my pastor and stated "I have to have the money by six o'clock tonight or I'll be evicted." He sounded desperate. After a few unsuccessful calls to verify his referral from my pastor—and not knowing I was being manipulated—I agreed to help him. I told him I could write out a church check to his landlord, but he said that his landlord only accepted cash. I told him that giving cash was not possible. He repeated his landlord's need for cash-only until I relented and gave in to his request. I did not want to disappoint this person, this stranger, so I agreed to give him cash. And, not only did I agree to give him cash, I agreed to leave it in an envelope for him at a downtown bar! My desire to please this stranger overshadowed the need for common sense and wisdom. What I did, essentially, was feed the requester's heroin habit (I read in the newspaper a few days later that he had been arrested for possession of drugs).

At that time, mercy meant giving. I did not consider or question the responsibility of the requester, nor did I think about how the money would be used. Giving made me feel good. I didn't know then about being "wise as serpents and innocent as doves" (Matt.10:16). Today, I have learned to follow Jesus wisely and not be manipulated by guilt or the tyranny of the urgent. I have learned that *not everything that cries the loudest is the most urgent.*

Setting boundaries

How do we balance the need presented with the need to evaluate the request? Is the need an interruption to our own agenda or an opportunity to serve in the name of Jesus? When do we say "yes," and when do we say "no"? How can we be most loving in the moment? How can we love ourselves and our neighbors at the same time? Where do we set the boundaries?

Listen to this heartbreaking story of a young woman who in the beginning thought service meant accepting any and all demands on her time and energy. Her tale describes how people were always dropping in and staying into the wee hours of the morning. Her relationship with her husband and children suffered because she was always physically and emotionally exhausted. She admits:

> I became the dumping place for preschoolers until I was just about berserk from the responsibility. I became the maker of clothes for many of the women who were working outside the home and simply did not have enough time to sew. I became the "listener" who spent so much time on the phone that there were many days when my children's lunches were fixed from things I could reach from the phone and my housework was untouched due to serving others. And on and on it went until I finally cracked, put my foot down and learned to say "no."[30]

Many church pastors have also learned to say, "no." Gordon MacDonald describes a phone call he received one Saturday morning. The woman's voice at the other end sounded very upset.

> "I've got to see you right away," she said. When I learned her name, I quickly realized that I had never met this person before and that she had rarely ever visited our church. "What is

the reason that we have to visit right now?" I asked. It was an important question, one of several I've learned through experience to ask. "My marriage is breaking up," she responded. I then asked, "When did you become aware that it was going to break up?" She answered, "Last Tuesday." I asked another question, "How long do you think the process of breaking up has been going on?" Her next comment was unforgettable. "Oh, it's been coming for five years." I managed to muffle my reaction and said, "Since you've seen this coming for five years, and since you knew it was going to happen since last Tuesday, why is it important to visit me at this moment?" She answered, "Oh, I had some free time this afternoon." Most of my time was accounted for; so I said, "I can understand why you think you have a serious problem. I'm going to propose that you call me Monday morning when we can arrange a time where my mind is in better shape. But that's not possible this afternoon. How does that sound?" She thought it was a terrific idea and could see why I suggested this sort of plan.[31]

MacDonald said that they both hung up reasonably happy. The caller would get to speak with him and he would protect his time from the "tyranny of the urgent." The principle again is that not everything that cries the loudest is the most urgent thing.

Do not be taken in by the con artist

Many people come to me for help in my capacity as Mercy Minister at Tenth Presbyterian Church. Ninety-five percent of these men and women I have not met before (and I have had contact with thousands of homeless and addicted men and women). The "word on the street" is that Tenth Presbyterian Church is an easy mark—they will say "yes" to any request. Most requests are tyranny of the urgent cries which sound like,

"You are my last hope. If you don't help me I'm going to die." What con artists want is to get hard cash or something that can be quickly sold for cash. Some people use "shock" value to turn us to helping them (one person dropped his pants to show me an area which needed medical attention). My job is to discern which needs are legitimate and which are "cons."

Over the many years I have served at Tenth Presbyterian Church—and years prior to that—I have been "taken" and "conned" by some very good actors and manipulative persons. Because of that I have developed, with the help of others, a list of rules:

1. Do not give money.
2. Do not give money.
3. When in doubt see rule #1.
4. Do not enter into a conversation with anyone smelling of beer or alcohol or whose eyes are bloodshot. Persons who are under the influence of a controlled substance may be boisterous or violent. Seek to peacefully escort these persons out of the church while speaking to them in a calm and gentle manner. Never touch or physically seek to maneuver a person. Standing to the side in a non-confrontational manner, state that they must leave or you will contact the police to escort them out (ask someone to dial 911).

No list of precautions is ever going to replace the element of compassion and judgment that must enter into every decision. I offer these precautions with the hope that my experience might be helpful to you. Here are a few guidelines I have developed:

1. Be aware that all drug addicts are pathological liars. They are totally controlled by the god of heroin or cocaine or ice or PCP or whatever they choose as their drug of choice.

2. Be wary of people who volunteer irrelevant information. People will bring an overwhelming number of receipts bundled together (e.g., hotel receipts, bus ticket stubs, hospital wrist band, applications, etc.) in order to bolster a story and create an aura of credibility. Most of the time they will unload their paperwork on your desk but not allow time for you to actually read any of it (if you did, it would be obvious that the receipts are old, dated and maybe not even in the name of the requester). One man's story was that he came to Philly for a job, was mugged in Independence Mall and everything was stolen—wallet, ID, money, backpack and an Olympus 3030-Z camera. He needed to get home to Pittsburgh. Yet that month several others used the exact same story. Never was the destination city different, and the camera model was always the same.

3. In the same way, be wary of people who offer an abundance of specific details. One person needed a wick for his kerosene heater. He told me heater model, its serial number, how much it cost and where the wick was on sale. He said it was only available at one hardware store (located conveniently near his residence) and if we gave him the cash he would be happy to save us the trouble of our buying the wick for him. I knew the person was an addict and I said that I could not help him. Later, he called another pastor while I was in his office. The request was the same although he used a different name. When the other pastor said, "You should really speak with David Apple," the requester hung up. (Please note that churches have a limited amount of resources and we want to be good stewards of those resources. Yes, we refuse to help some people. But

with the hundreds of homeless men and women we have relationships with, we help those who are really seeking to get their lives in order and want Jesus "to do business with their addictions").

4. Be wary of people who name-drop. Some people have seeming familiarity with highly regarded persons or with persons or agencies known to you. One person gave me a song and dance about being referred to me by one of the church deacons. He did not know that it is common practice for the deacons to give me a written referral if they are sending someone for help. When I asked which deacon referred him he said, "David Apple." On another occasion I received a call from someone named Mike who told me the office of the Philadelphia Presbytery referred him. Mike said, "Thank you for taking my call. I need your help. My name is Mike and I live in California. I'm attending a funeral in Philly and, well, I ran out of money and my credit cards are maxed out. I need $86 to pay my hotel bill or they will evict me. I have nowhere else to stay or store my twelve pieces of luggage. I haven't been able to get into a shelter—I called all the shelters and they can't help me. Can you help me? Listen, I'm using a borrowed phone which I have to return in just three minutes. What do you say? Will you help me? It is the end of a business day and no one can help me. No one wants to help a Christian." There were so many "red flags" in his comments telling me the request was bogus. How many did you count?

5. Be wary of people who forget or are otherwise unable to produce a "key" fact, the missing link necessary to corroborate their story. The requester might say that he is

really stressed out because of his circumstances and can't remember something vitally important. "The information is at the tip of my tongue but I can't find it." Then he will say, "You've got to believe me." Why do I?

6. Be wary of people who partially answer questions, attempt to shift the subject, seem not to hear key questions or pretend by mumbling to have a speech and hearing problem. They seem to be able to communicate their need to you, but then falter when you question them.

7. Similarly, be wary of people who place blocks inhibiting the verification of their story. You may hear the phrases, "This is really embarrassing and hard to talk about" or "This must be dealt with in absolute confidentiality" or "You can't say anything about this to anyone."

8. Be wary of people who stress the urgency of the request. Someone might say she has to have help now or by four o'clock today or she will suffer in some way. Others use children as bait and will bring photos which may be someone else's kids. People will come at five or six o'clock on a Friday afternoon—after all the social service agencies have closed—demanding help.

9. Be wary of people who always manipulate suggested solutions back to their terms. Usually this means that they must have immediate cash and no other solution will do. Once while I was walking to work, a man fell in step by step with me and asked for help to get food. I said I would be happy to give him my lunch but he was quick to tell me that he had food allergies. When I offered to go to the neighborhood grocery and buy what he needed, he said they didn't stock what he could eat. So I said,

"I guess I can't help you." Seeing that he could not con me, he walked off to try his story on someone else. FYI, I encourage people to carry an extra orange or banana to offer (nothing hard as many have bad teeth).

10. Be wary of people who attempt to produce a sense of guilt in us for doubting their honesty. Crying, tears flowing: "How could you not believe me? I thought you were a Christian. The church is supposed to help people like me." Are we supposed to give them whatever they want?

11. Be wary of who you let into your office. Many times it is wiser to speak in public or on the sidewalk if you sense trouble.

12. Be wary of people who appeal to our desire to play an important role in a significant story. "I have been to every church. No one will help me. I know you understand my dilemma and you look like I can trust you to help me." People pleasers will generally want to "help" rather than have the con artist not like them.

People whose needs are legitimate will rarely exhibit any of these characteristics, while con artists will show signs of all or most of them. The interesting thing is when I want to know where to go for a particular need, I ask a friend who still lives on the street. They know. It's their "job" to know how to survive.

Ministers, deacons and others can take some precautions from becoming a victim to the con artist by following these principles:

1. What was rule #1? Don't give money. The policy of our church is not to give money. This applies to members and regular attenders as well. Our church policy states that help be made available "in kind" and that no cash be used.

2. Determine what the need is. Is it spiritual? Material?

3. Seek to set up appointments with people. This will eliminate people whose needs are not legitimate and will protect your time. Those with genuine needs will return. I'd say that only one out of every ten return for their appointment.

4. Don't act impulsively. Wait. Don't do anything without thinking. Delay your response. Think about the story. Is it plausible? Does it sound manipulative to you? Do you feel that the requester has an ulterior motive—another use for the money? Also determine the best resources already available to help your guest. These are listed online—by zip code—by Salvation Army, United Way and denominational social service agencies. Make sure public and private agencies are being good stewards of God's resources. Discover ministry models that work and get to know the "gatekeepers" in those ministries and neighborhood associations. Don't duplicate what is out there already. Don't reinvent the wheel. Whenever possible, provide a Christ-centered alternative.

5. Determine what the person has done to help him or herself in the last day, week, month. What resources has he/she made use of? Why did this person come to you at this time?

6. Don't work harder than the people who come for help. You don't want to develop another dependency. Seek to motivate and empower them to help themselves. If you are making a referral, give them the phone number, the agency to call and the name of a contact person (if

you have it) and let them make the call. This is a small successful step, but a successful step nonetheless.

7. Remember, "No" is not a dirty word. More than a few people who come to our church "for help" are drug addicted or need immediate cash for some other illicit purpose. After years of being "soft" we are now up-front with requesters, stating very clearly what we will and will not do. As a matter of fact, con artists—who are very adept at time management—appreciate very much our coming right out to say we are not able to help in the way requested. That provides them with more time to try and con another person at another church.

8. Don't duplicate services that others provide. There are several churches in Tenth's neighborhood. At one time we all had a food and clothing closet. We found that the same people were hitting all the churches and some were selling our food to a grocer to support their drug habits. Since our food and clothing closet was redundant, we stopped providing that service. Now we make appropriate referrals to the other churches (one of them also does a thorough social service screening which is very helpful).

9. Check with other churches in your area. Have they received similar or identical requests? Con artists usually "make the rounds" going from church to church until someone says "no."

10. Be wary of people who want to "get out of town." Transportation tickets can be exchanged for cash even when we ask that they be stamped "nonrefundable." Travelers Aid is the appropriate agency for legitimate requests of this kind.

11. Pursue every means to avoid using cash. Make prior arrangements with local grocers and other merchants to use prepaid church "vouchers" or gift certificates that cannot be cashed or used to buy cigarettes, lottery tickets or alcoholic beverages.

12. Practice saying, "I'm sorry, I am not able to do that." By doing so, you will save yourself time (and if you are dealing with con artists, they will appreciate their time not being wasted too). If the requester knows that your answer is an emphatic "no," that person will leave.

13. Experience is a great teacher. We want to show compassion. We also want to protect our time, the church's money and resources and hold people accountable for their actions. We have learned to do what we do best—becoming involved, providing hospitality, establishing relationships and offering hope—so we specialize in that.

14. Try not to rescue people. There are natural consequences to people's actions. We can't save people but we can bring people into contact with the One who does save, Jesus.

15. Do not take too much responsibility for solving other people's problems. The Lord has given people a lot of resources to deal with their problems, therefore explore what resources they have and ask the person what they can do to mobilize those resources. Sometimes people get themselves into problem situations because they are acting irresponsibly and want someone to come in and make everything okay. Your job in these cases is to listen graciously, help as you can and then encourage people to take more responsibility for themselves.

16. Remember that you cannot change anyone. That is the business of the Holy Spirit. The only person you can change is yourself. If your efforts to aid someone appear to be unsuccessful in that he or she has not changed, remember that God is not done working in that person's life. Remember Mary, the drug addict who attended our Bible studies for ten years? We never saw her cooperate, never saw any fruit. All she wanted from us was material goods. All we got from her was grief. We finally asked her not to come back. A few years later I met her—clean and sober and a new person in Christ. God hadn't given up.

Preserving our time

I cannot direct attention enough to that waster of our time, energy, money and other resources: the tyranny of the urgent. Resist it. Not every interruption needs immediate attention. Not every interruption is an opportunity to help. People in need think that their immediate need is the most important thing in the world. It is not. Some things are important but not urgent. We need to keep our own agendas and try to accommodate others when appropriate and possible. Therefore, we need to schedule appointments with requesters for later times. When needs are genuine, people will return for their appointments. Over ninety percent of those who come for help do not return when given an appointment. Their needs are not genuine.

The reason we tend to give in to other people's urgent requests is that we want to please them. Our job is to please the Lord and do His will, not to win popularity contests. If we think that our job is to rescue people, we will be subject to every urgent appeal for help. Our job is to come alongside people in need, encourage them, pray with them and point them to Jesus. To resist the tyranny of the urgent, we need to have a good, prayerful sense of where the Lord wants us to focus our energies and attention at any given time.

Here is a brief summary warning I give my volunteers who are working very closely with people in need:

> We don't have to do everything. We do need to set bound-aries. A boundary is a limit. Only God is infinite. We are finite and need to function within our built-in limits. When people are in distress, they are often completely absorbed by their problems. Sometimes they will try to enmesh us in their problems, too. We cannot be effective helpers if we succumb to this. One question to ask ourselves is: "Where does my responsibility end and this person's begin (and vice versa)?

Self-preservation goes a long way. Saying "no" and setting other limits will protect us. Again, we are not required to deal with everything that comes our way. Some things are our le-gitimate responsibility. Other things will just siphon off our en-ergy, use up our time and leave us too drained to do what we should be doing. Knowing the signs of people consumers—those people who use, manipulate and drain us—are a means of self-preservation.

Knowing what resources are available is another help. Do not reinvent the wheel. There are often agencies or ministries that exist to solve the problems that people bring to you. Refer people to the appropriate agency that exists to deal with that very problem. And do not work harder than the person coming to you for help! Denying self does not mean destroying self.

9

The Role of the Deacon
in the Reformation and Today

John Calvin sought to provide help to the citizens of his sixteenth-century city. The role of the deacon in today's Reformed and Presbyterian churches was established by this Protestant Reformer. For Calvin, the intentional partnering of worship with ethics, and love of God with love of neighbor was biblical and necessary. For Calvin, ministry was the work of the Holy Spirit in the life of the believer and Scripture was authoritative for faith and practice, regeneration and transformation.

Calvin believed that all the faithful should care for their neighbors, and that the church should give specific leadership to this common Christian duty. In 1557 he wrote a letter to the churches in Geneva. In it, he said, "Let us raise in each member of the Christian community the spiritual problem of his material life, of his goods, of his time, and of his capabilities, in view of freely putting them at the service of God and neighbor."[32]

The church in Geneva was not originally concerned with the distribution of alms or with any other means to care for the material needs of Geneva's citizenry. It was largely the work of Calvin that changed this. Calvin structured a society where the poor could be cared for through the office of deacon. According to theologian Benjamin Warfield, the governing authority of Geneva was helping the poor, but the church of Geneva was not.

"When I first came to this Church," Calvin says, "there was as good as nothing here. . . . There was preaching and that was all." He would have found much the same state of things everywhere else in the Protestant world. The Church in the early Protestant conception was constituted by the preaching of the Word and the right administration of the sacraments: the correction of morals was the concern not of the Church but of the civil power. . . . Calvin could not take this view of the matter. "Whatever others may hold," he observed, "we cannot think so narrowly of our office that when preaching is done our task is fulfilled, and we may take our rest." In his view the mark of a true Church is not merely that the gospel is preached in it, but that it is "followed."[33]

Reform movements

With simultaneous movements of Reformation and Renaissance, there was a reform of many inadequate and wrong kinds of relief for the poor. Calvin was one of many refugees living in Geneva hoping that someday all of France would be evangelized and that the Reformed religion would be allowed to prosper freely. Awaiting that day, he and his friends in this border city provided for the continuing stream of Protestant refugees from Roman Catholic areas by offering them food and shelter. This hospitality was known as the *Bourse Francaise*—"the French fund for poor foreigners"—intended for those who came to Geneva to live according to the "reform of the Word."[34]

Calvin was familiar with the history of the early church and its relationship to the poor. The church had always been an advocate of the disadvantaged and Christians in the early church took care of their own and others as well. Emperor Julian of Rome is quoted, "Nothing has contributed more to the progress of the superstition of the Christians as their charity to strangers. . . . The impious Galileans provide not only for their own poor, but for ours as well."[35]

The early church also fed the poor, nursed the sick, housed the homeless and rescued those who were abandoned and left to die. The bourse showed concrete examples of Calvin's modeling these actions, revealing that he not only preached charity but generously supported the poor as well. Martin Bucer also gave service to mankind a fundamental place in his theology. For Bucer, Jesus' acts of mercy are signs of the kingdom of God breaking in. He said *diakonia* also is a sign of the church in addition to the proclamation of the Word and the sacraments.[36]

By 1535, the cry for social reform sprang from many divergent groups. First the scholastic reformers spoke of the need to channel new life into social care. They wanted to redirect money and goods away from corrupt ministers and divert it into the hands of pious laymen for distribution to the poor. They also sought to develop a system of civic safeguards to ensure the proper administration of public charity. Mercy, service and giving became an inescapable responsibility for Protestants. Using God's gifts properly played a prominent part in Calvin's thinking about service and love for others. He said, "All the gifts we possess have been bestowed by God and entrusted to us on condition that they be distributed for our neighbor's benefit."[37]

He believed that all Christians are stewards of everything God has provided them, and as such, are required to give an accounting of how we have loved our neighbors.

Calvin's diaconate

The Reformers brought needed change in the way gifts were made in support of the poor. New patterns of benevolence emerged in response to the scriptural mandate for diaconal ministry. The Reformers reversed the unbiblical habit of churchgoers giving alms to the poor to earn merits against years in purgatory (a Roman Catholic teaching). The Reformers taught that giving was the believer's response of love to God and to their neighbor. Calvin said,

> For the Christian, the act of offering is an essential spiritual act, an act of worship in the highest degree. Indeed by his offering the believer certifies to God that Mammon has been dethroned. By concrete gifts, the Christian expresses to God the real measure of his faith. By these gifts, the man confesses that his Lord is really to be acknowledged master of his entire life—moral, physical and material.[38]

Calvin believed that any task to glorify God and serve a neighbor is ministry. He stated, "It is clear . . . that love of neighbor is the most unmistakable evidence of our love for God, so it is essential that the Church have a diaconal office and not leave this religious duty only to individual Christians or civil authority."[39]

Accordingly, Calvin looked to Scripture for inspiration and explanation for what he did. He believed that the church's charity went beyond meeting physical needs only, but spiritual needs as well. Charity was not just philanthropic; it was a reflection of the Christian life and the Christian community incorporated into the daily life of the city. He did not believe that poverty could be entirely eliminated, but this did not immobilize him. He condemned the world for disorder and sought a new order based on Scripture and obedience to the sovereignty of God.

For Calvin, biblical belief was a system—a blueprint for behavior, telling what a person should do or should not do in order to be humane and loving. To honor God went beyond the walls of buildings to service in the world. To worship God was to serve him in imitation of our Savior Jesus, who "came not to be served but to serve" (Matt. 20:28). Calvin believed that the temporal care of the poor was no less sacred than ecclesiastical activity. While the gathering for worship always took precedence, the love of our neighbor had to be an inevitable result. They were inseparable. He said that piety is the root of love. Piety shows our fear or reverence of God, but we also fear God when we live justly among our brethren.[40]

Calvin founded his diaconate on several verses of Scripture: Leviticus 19:9–10, Acts 6:1–6, 1 Timothy 3:8–13 and 5:3–10, Romans 12:8, 1 Corinthians 12:28; and on the character and life of our Lord Jesus Christ. These would describe the deacon, the character of the people who served the poor and the actual service of the Geneva diaconate: feed the poor, nurse the sick, house the homeless and rescue newborn and abandoned infants.

Speaking on 1 Timothy during a sermon series in 1554–55, Calvin expounded to his congregation that the diaconate is,

> Not at all an earthly office, but . . . a spiritual charge from God. They are not only in a public estate, but they belong to the spiritual regime of the Church, and they are there as God's officers. The deacons are chosen to be like the hands of God, and they are there in a sacred office.[41]

Calvin believed that Christians, having been bought with a price through the blood of Christ, belonged to God with all they are and all they own. He said,

> We are not our own: let not our reason nor our will, therefore, sway our plans and deeds. We are not our own: let us

therefore, not set it as our goal to seek what is expedient for us according to the flesh. We are not our own: insofar as we can, let us therefore forget about ourselves, and all that is ours. Conversely, we are God's; let us therefore live for him and die for him. We are God's: let his wisdom and his will therefore rule in our actions. We are God's: let all the parts of our life accordingly strive toward him as our only lawful goal.[42]

Belonging to God and being saved by grace through faith—not merit—gave Calvin great peace about life and freely serving others. According to Calvin, the doctrine of election was an unspeakable comfort because it eliminated all such worries and freed Christians from concern about themselves in order that they might "devote every energy to the unflagging service of the sovereign Lord."[43] This was expressed in the service shown by the deacons especially.

The office of deacon fell right into the existing institution of hospitals. The *Hôpital-Général* was a religious mission as well as medical and social. Calvin ordained the hospital officers (pro-curers) and *hospitaliers* (deacons). The hospitals united both the religious and the practical.

The largest numbers in the hospital were children who were orphans of the plagues, abandoned or illegitimate. They received a basic education in reading and writing. Boys were apprenticed at thirteen years of age and also worked in the fields. Girls of thirteen years could become servants to respectable families and dowries were put up for girls intended for marriage. The next largest group was the aged and widows who had no money or family. The hospital cared for those whose only option was to accept charity. Those who were not sickly worked on the grounds, in the fields, performed household duties, made repairs and cared for the sick. The third group consisted of the blind, crippled, weak, physically and mentally ill and pregnant women. Ordinances sought to outlaw begging. Healthy beggars had to work and those who could not were supported by the church without shame and the temptation to beg.

Two kinds of deacons

For Calvin "There have always been two kinds [of deacons] in the early Church: one to receive, distribute and care for the goods of the poor, the other to tend and look after the sick."[44]

Deacons visited the poor and sick, distributed money and gifts in kind. They kept strict accounts for all disbursements and for the managed, rented and kept houses they used in ministry. The deacon according to Calvin, and later the Reformed Church, was an ecclesiastical minister whose duty was to care for the poor through benevolence individually or in cooperation with the local authorities. Calvin accepted the possibility of the church's diaconate cooperating with a civil welfare program.

As mentioned before, for Calvin involvement in his city was not peripheral to worship and faith. He made a consistent challenge to his hearers. Calvin was much concerned, as physician of souls, to combat the human indolence, drowsiness, dullness, coldness, the various signs that we are, in life, already half dead.[45]

He believed that Christians are under God's reign and that they must reform religion and society. He sought a new order secured through obedience to God. For Calvin, society existed to serve fundamental human needs. The basis of a Christian society, for Calvin, was a constant awareness of others deeply rooted in the heart of Christ. And this community was to be rooted firmly in the gospel and equipped for every good work. Karl Barth said this about the sixteenth century reformer's ministry paradigm:

We accept Calvin as an example or as a model only in the measure in which he has, in an unforgettable way, pointed out to the Church of his time the road to obedience: obedience of thought and deeds. . . . An authentic and true follower of Calvin has only one road to follow: obeying not Calvin himself but the one who was the master of Calvin.[46]

The role of the deacon today

In seeking to follow Christ, today's church is challenged to develop a new paradigm for Christ-centered mercy ministry. Many people pass by houses of worship believing that they are not relevant to their needs. For many, God is not an option because the church itself is not a witness of Jesus' love and concern. For the church to be seen as credible and relevant by those living in its community it needs to actively demonstrate this through mercy and service. What it does demonstrate all too often is not representing the loving compassion of Christ. It shows the harsh coldness of earlier Greek society where being served was more dignified than serving. As Plato wrote, "How can a man be happy when he has to serve someone?"[47] To the ancient Greek, service had a lowly position. To be true to that culture was to have little or no concern for the needs of others.

The Greek position is completely opposed to the attitude Jesus possessed and the one He requires for His followers. Philippians 2:5–8 speaks about the humility of Christ—our attitude should be the same as that of Christ Jesus. In Romans 12, Paul indicates that valuing others—putting them first—is important. He writes to the church, "By the mercies of God, present your bodies as a living sacrifice." They are not to "be conformed to this world . . . " and they are to "be transformed by the renewal of [their] mind." The entire New Testament makes clear that love which stops short of practical help is "in word only" or simply "of the tongue" and a denial of the Lord we serve. The Reformers reminded us that the absence of obedience is a sign of disbelief.

The church is the body of Christ representing Him in the world. The apostle Paul tells us in 1 Corinthians 12:27, "You are the body of Christ and individually members of it." The late theologian Lewis Smedes, in a booklet on diaconal ministry, says, "The Church is Jesus Christ bodily present, bodily committed to, and bodily immersed in the ghetto of human history. The Church, His body, still carries on [his] work. . . . And it is vulnerable, open to wounds, because it, with Him, is still part of the [human] ghetto."[48]

It is this Jesus, the divine Deacon, who taught us how to serve using the diversity of gifts described in Romans 12:4–8:

> For as in one body we have many members, and the members do not all have the same function, so we, though many, are one body in Christ, and individually members one of another. Having gifts that differ according to the grace given to us, let us use them: if prophecy, in proportion to our faith; if service, in our serving; the one who teaches, in his teaching; the one who exhorts, in his exhortation; the one who contributes, in generosity; the one who leads, with zeal; the one who does acts of mercy, with cheerfulness.

This reference is not simply to differences of character or personality type, which in Christ achieves a mysterious unity. The reference is more of a "diversity of function. As the hand, foot, eye, mouth, etc., each performs the function which makes for a total life and action of the body; so do the members of the body of Christ function toward the fullness of Christ's service to the world."[49]

Diakonia is the principle by which our Lord describes His entire ministry, and of the life and ministry of His followers:

> Everything that was done by the Son of Man who came, Jesus Christ, including humiliation, self-emptying, cross and death is summarized in eight letters: *d i a k o n i a.* The same single word also indicates the pattern of life for all who followed Jesus. *Diakonia:* they go into service. . . . They are other-directed. . . . They find themselves among those in need; it has become their natural milieu. . . . They discover that they are being drawn into Jesus' diaconate and start participating in it.[50]

Diakonia is essential for the life and well-being of the Church. The diaconate is about what the church is or should be. It is not something optional to the main thrust of the church's ministry, but stands at the heart of the gospel and its mission to the world. It is a reasoned and biblical concern for the well-being of another. Those concerned with diaconal ministry are not merely concerned that no one is without food, but, also, about encouraging members and ensuring that they lack no good thing. They should be concerned that each member of the church has a place, feels cared for and can function according to the gifts each has been given.

Ways deacons serve

Ministry of mercy and compassion not only includes taking care of the financially poor, but also to relieving other forms of oppression and affliction. Yet, so many ordained servants enter compassion ministry without training or experience. They literally don't know what to do and don't understand the scope of their job description. Here, listed alphabetically (not in importance) are numerous ways diaconates serve their members. They presently care for these ministries:

- Benevolence
- Building and grounds
- Communion
- Counseling
- Fellowship
- Financial matters
- Hospital visitation
- Outreach to nonmembers
- Outreach to members who are poor, sick, elderly, widowed, orphaned and have special needs
- Worship management, ushering, greeting and security

This is a lengthy description of responsibilities, and the majority of diaconates do it all themselves. But this is not a healthy model. I believe the healthy and appropriate model for deacons is described by Luke in Acts 6:1–3. The text reads:

> Now in these days when the disciples were increasing in number, a complaint by the Hellenists arose against the Hebrews because their widows were being neglected in the daily distribution. And the twelve summoned the full number of the disciples and said, "It is not right that we should give up preaching the word of God to serve tables. Therefore, brothers, pick out from among you seven men of good repute, full of the Spirit and of wisdom, whom we will appoint to this duty.

Although these seven were not called deacons here, they performed a diaconal ministry of mercy and service.

The ministry to which they were called was caring for Grecian widows who were being neglected in this growing Christian community. At the time, there were hundreds of new converts in the Hebrew-, Aramaic- and Greek-speaking synagogues and the apostles were overwhelmed (according to Acts 2:41, three thousand were converted on one day). And, for "the seven," what were the biblical requirements for this new ministry? Luke records that each must have a good reputation—filled with the Holy Spirit and wisdom—to be able to manage this new ministry of caring for the Greek-speaking widows. Picture this: there were hundreds of widows living within Jerusalem's walls and in the countryside, and a mere seven men who were called to serve. They, literally, could not do it all by themselves (as the apostles could not preach and serve). They needed the Holy Spirit and wisdom to manage and delegate such a ministry.

How deacons respond to current ministry

Similarly, consider today's diaconal responsibilities of benevolence, building and grounds, caring for those in need, communion, counseling, fellowship, financial counseling, outreach, visitation, worship management, ushering, greeting and security. During my diaconal consultations, deacons have raised the following issues:

1. "We are very disorganized and need organization skills." Included in their complaints are not knowing what resources are available nor how to refer people or to whom they should refer. As one deacon said, "Everything is beyond our expertise!"

2. At another church, the discussion focused on the problem of time constraints. The deacons were not available during the day from Monday to Friday. A solution to caring for others during that time was also unavailable to

them. "How can we involve others in mercy ministry [or in "our" mercy ministry]? How can we expose and train others when we feel undertrained ourselves?"

3. "We oversee both mercy ministry and the building. It is difficult to get volunteers to help us."

During other discussions, I've heard questions such as these:

1. "What must we do as deacons?" Many churches provide no training prior to deacons being elected and taking office. It almost seems like these churches require no more than the person be breathing.

2. "What is our biblical responsibility in the church and to the community?" The lack of biblical knowledge frightens them and leads only to frustration, burnout and occasionally, deacons leaving the church. That is a sad commentary.

3. "What is not our responsibility?" Underneath this question is the premise that deacons don't have to do everything.

4. "What resources are available for our use and referral?" A simple community survey or a walk/ride around the neighborhood will answer this question.

5. "What ministries do neighboring churches have that we either complement or duplicate?" Again, asking the right people the right questions will give you the answers you need.

6. "How can we stop feeling like we are putting out fires all over the place?" Only when people realize that there is a problem and do something to solve it will things change for the better. It takes more than doing the same

problem-producing activity over and over again, expecting different results. That's insane.

Tenth's diaconal survey

Because deacons at Tenth were asking similar questions
over the years, we did a study of our own diaconate and compared our findings with how other church diaconates operate.
Our committee contacted six PCA churches: New City Fellowship, Saint Louis, Missouri; Briarwood Presbyterian Church,
Birmingham, Alabama; Perimeter Church, Atlanta, Georgia;
First Presbyterian Church (First Pres.), Jackson, Mississippi; Redeemer Presbyterian Church, New York, New York; Proclamation Presbyterian Church, Bryn Mawr, Pennsylvania; plus Park
Street Church, Boston, Massachusetts; and Capitol Hill Baptist Church, Washington DC. These churches represent big and
small; North, South, Midwest and East Coast; urban and suburban. The twenty-question survey focused on how the diaconates
are organized, type of training provided, workload demands,
diaconal guidelines and benevolence issues.

1.   Organization

   a.   Structure: Briarwood and New City have full-time paid
        diaconal staff who help coordinate their mercy/benevo-
        lence ministry and work closely with the diaconal offi-
        cers. The focus of New City, Capitol Hill, Perimeter and
        Briarwood care ministries is their Sunday and midweek
        group meetings.

   b.   Delegation/use of gifts: Many of the church's deacons
        delegate worship service tasks so they may worship and
        otherwise focus on mercy and benevolence (Capitol Hill:
        "They are coordinators, not do-ers"). Two churches give

their deacons every other month off. Those who delegate state that ministry is more manageable and ministry fatigue a thing of the past. Capitol Hill seeks to equip (developing a culture for service) so members act when they see someone hurting and contact the officers if the help needed is beyond what they can give.

c. Encouragement/Support: The more contact the deacons have with leadership, the more encouraged they are. This is especially true where there are full-time diaconal staff or elders who meet regularly with the deacons for team building, listening and encouragement (First Pres., Briarwood and New City).

d. Recruitment: These churches have no official nominating committees. Recruitment is mostly done through relationships established in community groups, clusters and ministry groups. Redeemer stated that they need more deacons; First Pres. wished they could double the number of deacons to provide better congregation care.

e. Terms: Most have three-year terms with a necessary year off. New City and First Pres. have no terms—deacons serve out of their passion for ministry and take time off as needed.

2. Training

a. Preparation for new officers: Training is required at each of the churches prior to assuming office. At Briarwood, "Training (ten weeks) and delegation have rejuvenated the diaconate;" First Pres., eight weeks; New City, four courses plus one year as deacon-in-training; Proclamation, one day leadership training; Redeemer, four weeks mercy and theology; Perimeter, Theological Foundations course. Capitol Hill and Park Street assign their deacons to specific ministries with specialized training.

b. Ongoing training/refresher courses: Briarwood and Redeemer have training/team building portions at monthly meetings; all but Proclamation have annual refresher courses.

c. Support: Relationships and trust is an intentional key factor at New City; eating together with the elders monthly assists Redeemer's and Perimeter's deacons. At Briarwood the officers work together in their Congregational Communities.

3.   Making Workload Manageable

a. Worship: Most churches rely heavily on volunteers. At First Pres., deacons only serve at one of the three services (all similar to Tenth in size). Redeemer and New City deacons have no responsibilities for the worship service. These deacons are available to meet with members in need every Sunday.

b. Meetings: Most diaconates meet monthly. Briarwood's and New City's meet every other month and New City's executive committee meets as needed. Redeemer and Briarwood spend time with the Session during their meeting night.

c. Mercy: The southern churches have strong women's mercy ministries. These assist the deacons in work with widows, bereavement, single moms and benevolence. At the other churches deacons coordinate ministries, but seek to make good use of members' time and talents (similar to ACTS at Tenth). Capitol Hill's goal is unity in the body. To accomplish this, the pastors work to "prepare and equip for works of service." Also, many have been trained in Christian counseling.

d. Communion: At several churches, deacons have no responsibilities here. Others coordinate/delegate preparation of elements. Most celebrate communion quarterly or bimonthly. Perimeter uses a user-friendly automatic tray-cup dispenser for its weekly evening service. At First Pres., the same volunteer family has prepared the elements for years.

e. Women and service: Most of the churches interviewed have a high view of the priesthood of all believers. Although the southern churches do not have deaconesses, women are organized for much congregational care.

4. Guidelines

a. Decision making: Most of the churches have empowered deacons to make decisions concerning benevolence without committee approval. This means one can approve up to $200, two can approve $400, etc. At Redeemer, two can approve $2000, three-$3000, five-$5000.

b. Budgeting for benevolence: Briarwood and New City have purposed to spend the money allocated annually for benevolence. New City had thirty-five cents left in its account at the end of the year. Briarwood stated, "We want to give!"

5. Benevolence Issues

a. Long-term: Overall, long-term cases are difficult for every church. Redeemer stated, "We are troubled by long-term cases—how to motivate people." First Pres.,

"How do you balance love and limits? We don't have any written guidelines here. We have good men who oversee these financial resources, and they attempt to do so in a God-honoring, compassionate and wise manner."

b. General: At Redeemer, the deacons focus on benevolence, advocacy and prayer. Each deacon feels burdened by having five active cases. They need more deacons. "Client change is too slow. People need help with work/lifestyle transition. There are more marital struggles. . . ."

c. Combating compassion fatigue/burnout: Briarwood has an elder on the mercy committee to provide encouragement and, also, a mercy pastor on staff to assist the deacons and lighten their load. This is true at New City which has a full-time administrative deacon. And both of these churches assign deacons according to their gifts. Briarwood has thirty mercy deacons and ninety-six administrative deacons. At Capitol Hill most of the care is done by the members.

6. Improvement Needed

a. Capitol Hill stated that their elders need to disciple the deacons more; First Pres. recognizes that some folks are falling between the cracks; Perimeter sees the need to include opportunity for more fellowship/camaraderie in the diaconate; Proclamation indicated that everyone is too busy and the level of commitment needs improvement; Park Street said that better leadership is needed.

7. Recommendations for Tenth

a. Redevelop/redefine the Director of Mercy Ministries job description to benefit Tenth's diaconate and diaconal ministry through training, cooperation and consultation. (Done)

    i. Help develop a working partnership between the deacons and the director of Mercy Ministry. (Done)

b. Develop new training curriculum.

    i. Require that all deacons and diaconal candidates take training classes. (Done)

    ii. Make sure they are prepared to serve in advance of installation. (Done)

c. Develop new guidelines.

    i. Shift the deacon paradigm from doing to coordinating/facilitating. (Progressing)

    ii. Give the deacons more power to make decisions on their own as they seek to serve those in need. (Done)

    iii. Allow them to serve according to their gifts.

d. Make equipping the saints a priority. (Progressing)

    i. Make better use of volunteers.

    ii. Free up the deacons for more service of benevolence/mercy.

e. Map Tenth's most vulnerable members on a geographic grid so they don't "fall between the cracks." (Progressing)

f. Seek ways to encourage and build up the deacons. (Progressing)

    i. Prevent ministry fatigue and burnout from the very beginning.

g. Make the parish system more workable. (Progressing)

i. Learn how Tenth can use the community models of Briarwood and Capitol Hill.

ii. Employ Tenth Women and other groups for greater service in the parishes.

iii. Identify what transferable service models are operating "unofficially" in the church/parish and empower them to use their gifts to the fullest.

The above survey indicated that all of the above churches were asking similar questions: 1) What tasks require the Holy Spirit and wisdom—that is, what must deacons do? 2) What tasks do not require the Holy Spirit and wisdom, meaning they can be delegated to others? This helped Tenth look at its own ministry paradigm and move to take initial steps to restructure the diaconate. As noted in the above recommendation, Tenth had done these or has it in progress.

A model of servant-leadership

During my years training deacons, I have heard many opinions regarding the role of the deacon. These include the many mentioned earlier. But, here is my list:

1. Deacons must equip and mobilize the saints.

2. Deacons must collect the gifts of God's people and distribute them.

3. Deacons must stimulate a diaconal lifestyle.

4. Deacons must come alongside those who are hurting.

5. Deacons must prevent poverty within the body.

6. Deacons must be knowledgeable about local community resources.

7. Deacons must empower the needy to make good use of all available institutions of mercy.

8. Deacons must cooperate with neighboring churches.

Note that these do not conform to the six statements below, that I use during my training. I jokingly begin our discussion with these:

1. A qualification of the office of deacon is the ability to put out many fires at the same time. (True or False)

2. A qualification of the office of deacon is the ability to be ruled by "The Tyranny of the Urgent." (True or False)

3. *The Book of Church Order* specifically prohibits deacons from having their voicemail intercept phone calls during family meals. Deacons must answer every call. (True or False)

4. According to 1 Timothy 24:7 deacons are charged to do all the work of the church. (True or False)

5. *The Book of Church Order* states that deacons must model for the congregation the various ways of burning out outlined by Elijah in 1 Kings 19. (True or False)

6. *The Westminster Confession of Faith* proscribes that deacons alone have personal responsibility to carry out their tasks. It is sinful to accept the help of others. (True or False)

The answer to all these is "False" (as you knew). All kidding aside, I believe the following show the role of the deacon.

Role #1: Deacons must equip and mobilize the saints.

One of the primary diaconal responsibilities is to teach the how-tos of diaconal ministry to church members. According to *The Book of Church Order of the Presbyterian Church in America*, "The office [of deacon] is one of sympathy and service after the example of the Lord Jesus. It expresses also the communion of saints, especially in their helping one another in time of need. It is the duty of the deacons to minister to those who are in need, to the sick, to the friendless and to any who may be in distress."[51]

It is not the deacons' task to be "Lone Rangers" in their ministry. Ephesians 4 calls for the equipping of the saints by church leaders. This means preparing Christians for service by giving them all they need to accomplish their tasks. The equipper is a master craftsman developing an apprentice. The equipper is a teacher educating a pupil. The equipper is a coach preparing a player and a team. The equipper is a doctor healing/restoring a patient. In the Gospel of Mark, the writer speaks of nets being mended before they can be used properly. Fishermen must check out their equipment before use and fix the nets when they need repair. That is the same equipping design for church leaders: ensure members are properly prepared prior to their serving others. Here is what the PCA Guidelines state:

> In view of the responsibility of the teaching office to equip the saints for ministry (Eph. 4:11–16), it would appear that the same principle should apply to diaconal leadership. While deacons do not have the shepherding and disciplining authority of elders, they do take the lead in the ministry of mercy. Acts 6:3 indicates that diaconal ministers should be full of spiritual wisdom, which is always the qualification for leadership (I Kings 3:7–11; cf. II Sam.14:17).[52]

As leaders, deacons should not only minister in the name of the church, but should encourage the church's body of believers by their example to fulfill the ministry of mercy and service to which the Lord calls all members. John 13:15 says, "I have given you an example, that you also should do just as I have done to you." For the health and maturity of the church, deacons must teach, equip and motivate members to serve in ministry. According to *The Book of Church Order*, "It is expedient that . . . a church should select and appoint godly men and women of the congregation to assist the deacons in caring for the sick, the widows, the orphans, the prisoners, and others who may be in any distress or need."[53]

For years, Tenth and ACTS have provided general diaconal training and training for ministry in nursing homes, prisons, hospitals and other institutions. We have also trained for single parents and divorce recovery ministry and serving those with special needs. And we have held general training to help everyone come alongside those in need.

Thus, teaching, equipping and motivating members to serve is vital. And the numbers involved will usually indicate the spiritual temperature of a congregation. Although the dictionary definition of the word volunteer is "One who enters into or offers himself for a service of his own free will," those who follow Christ are commanded to follow in an obedient walk.[54]

Christ says "If you love me, you will keep my commandments" (John 14:15). In other words, "If you say you will follow Me, then do as I do." *Deaconing* has to do with our lifestyle and our relationship with Jesus. The church needs to be those equipped with towels, ready to clean the wounds of those who suffer. We are called, as Jesus, to "bind up the brokenhearted" (Isa. 61:1). Deacons must stimulate church members to action— helping the body of believers follow their Master, who said that He came to serve (to deacon), not to be served (see Matt. 20:28).

Role #2: Deacons must collect the gifts of God's people and distribute them.

After stating that the deacon's task is ministering to those who are in need, to the sick, to the friendless and to any who may be in distress, *The Book of Church Order* continues, "It is their duty also to develop the grace of liberality in the members of the church, to devise effective methods of collecting the gifts of the people, and to distribute these gifts among the objects to which they are contributed."[55]

This seems so obvious, for scripture is clear on giving. Moses writes in Leviticus 27:30, "Every tithe of the land, whether of the seed of the land or of the fruit of the trees, is the LORD's; it is holy to the LORD." Luke tells us in Acts 4:32, "Now the full number of those who believed were of one heart and soul, and no one said that any of the things that belonged to him was his own, but they had everything in common." Paul shares in 2 Corinthians 8:4 and 14 that the saints begged "us earnestly for the favor of taking part in the relief of the saints." He says there should be a mutual concern for one another: "Your abundance at the present time should supply their need, so that their abundance may supply your need, that there may be fairness." In God's way, we Christians are only stewards of our financial possessions. We own nothing in any absolute sense as it all belongs to God. So obviously, Christians provide for the church through these offerings.

What is not as obvious or stated clearly enough in today's churches, however, is the need for Christians to also tithe their skills, talents and time to the church. These also belong to God. 1 Corinthians 6:20 says, "You were bought with a price." The *Heidelberg Catechism*, a creed of Reformed churches, opens with: "I am not my own, but belong unto my faithful Savior Jesus Christ. . . ."[56]

So, just as deacons facilitate the financial offerings of God's people, they must collect data on the talents of God's people—that is, they should develop a talent bank and a system to use these resources. Church leaders should not have to use guess-work to determine who is available when a particular service is needed—like who is available to bring Mrs. M for dialysis Wednesdays mornings at 8:30 or who can fix a senior member's toilet or who can do minor repairs for a member with special needs.

An inventory of gifts and talents should be at the church's fingertips—listing all the various vocations—lawyers, accountants, those in the building trade, beauticians, etc., those who have a truck and those who will just make themselves available. I also suggest a database of blood types so that in case of critical need, people can give the gift of life (see Appendix C). According to 1 Peter 4:10, "As each has received a gift, use it to serve one another, as good stewards of God's varied grace." Christians intentional giving of spiritual gifts, talents, vocational skills and time is an example of biblical stewardship. The apostle Paul commends this in 1 Corinthians 12:7, "To each is given the manifestation of the Spirit for the common good." And he reminds the church of its essential unity in Romans 12:5, "We, though many, are one body in Christ, and individually members one of another." In the New Testament every member of the church has received the gift of grace and has been called to service. The writer of Hebrews says "[God will] equip you with everything good that you may do his will, working in us that which is pleasing in his sight, through Jesus Christ, to whom be glory forever and ever" (13:21). 1 Corinthians 12:5 states that the gift of the Spirit's grace brings "varieties of service." Paul continues, "There are different kinds of service, but the same

Lord. There are different kinds of working, but the same God works all of them in all men (12:5–6, NIV 1984)."

Role #3: Deacons are to stimulate and model a servant lifestyle for the use of these gifts.

Deacons have a great opportunity, as catalysts, to give ministry away and share the blessings of serving. They can do that through mentoring others, on-the-job training and showing leadership by modeling the joy of service—they can out-zeal one another in zeal. As Romans 12:6–8 says, "Having gifts that differ according to the grace given to us, let us use them: . . . the one who leads, with zeal; the one who does acts of mercy, with cheerfulness."

As mentors, deacons would work alongside members, instructing and encouraging, careful to model the task at hand for the benefit of the member. Here the focus is not only on the task (mechanics), but confidence in the Lord and His service (obedience). Both cooperate to develop a fearless church worker. Adding to the ease of mentoring, members can personally select a mentor with whom they have prior experience or contact. Similarly, on-the-job training provides hands-on instruction in areas that do not require close inspection or instruction. In many cases it can be mastered merely from observation. Of course, each deacon will need to attend some form of "officer training school" to learn expertise in the knowledge of mentoring or by gaining the same through their own mentor-mentee relationship. Either way, they would teach *diakonia*, the principle by which our Lord describes His entire ministry and of the life and ministry of His followers.

Role #4: Deacons come alongside those who are hurting and serve the distressed with good counsel.

In one of my workshops, I use this cry for help: "I hurt and I feel there is no one there. No one I can talk to—no one who will listen—no one who will bear my burden. I feel lonely, fearful and sad. I feel tired and unwanted. I know there's something better—I'm about to give up. Will you help me? Could you come alongside me? But, can I trust you? Will you be condescending and humiliate me? Oh, I so need your help. Can you show me respect? Can you understand me without belittling me? Guide me without judging? Listen without dictating? Can you offer me hope? Can you live out God's love to me? Can you show that you really care?"

James 2:24 says, "You see that a person is justified by works and not by faith alone." He encourages us to "visit [care for] orphans and widows in their affliction" (1:27). Paul writes in 2 Corinthians 1:3–4, the "God of all comfort . . . comforts us in all our affliction, so that we may be able to comfort those who are in any affliction, with the comfort with which we ourselves are comforted by God." In order to give comfort, we need to be available to others and we need to take time to listen to what is occurring in the lives of those we seek to serve. The latter, listening with the desire to help, is probably the more difficult. In *Life Together*, Dietrich Bonhoeffer reminds us,

> Many people are looking for an ear that will listen. They do not find it among Christians, because these Christians are talking when they should be listening. But he who can no longer listen to his brother will soon be no longer listening to God. Anyone who thinks that his time is too valuable to spend keeping quiet will eventually have no time for God and his brother, but only for himself and for his own follies.[57]

We need to include in our agendas time for those in need and not ignore their suffering. Proverbs 18:14 says, "A man's spirit will endure sickness, but a crushed spirit who can bear?" And in Philippians 2:3–4, the apostle Paul shares, "Do nothing from selfish ambition or conceit, but in humility count others more significant than yourselves. Let each of you look not only to his own interests, but also to the interests of others." In order to comfort others, we have to get close to them and not be fearful of that contact. Henri Nouwen reminds us,

> We all need people who will not be too quick to take our pain away but will have the spiritual and mental toughness to walk with us, sharing in the journey to the point where woundedness can be confronted at its source. Shared woundedness becomes mobilizing. The sting is drawn because the secret is shared.[58]

I encourage deacons to be observant on Sundays. Be on the lookout for members who need help or have been prayed for during the week. "Seek them out," I say, "as you have the chance. Greet them, speak to, encourage and pray with them." This should be a visitation bringing hope and the basis for follow-up. At future diaconal meetings, each deacon can share how he or she brought hope and made a difference in someone's life.

Deacons are in a position to provide people with healthy fellowship and draw them into the unity of the church. They are catalysts for healing. By being with those who suffer, they are able to really help and not just help in the abstract.

Role #5: Deacons must seek to prevent poverty for church members.

Deacons need to keep an eye on their members, looking out for the most vulnerable—those who are poor, sick, elderly, fatherless and widowed—so that none fall between the cracks.

Deacons should not stop at feeding the hungry, clothing the naked and rescuing the oppressed in their midst. They need to use the church's spiritual and material resources and alleviate any members' poverty so that these brothers and sisters can function and be able to help others in the church's body of believers. In Ephesians 4:28 the apostle Paul indicates that one of the benefits of working and earning a living is to help those in need: "Let the thief no longer steal, but rather let him labor, doing honest work with his own hands, so that he may have something to share with anyone in need." *The Heidelberg Catechism* asks, "What does God require of you in the eighth commandment?" It answers, "That I further my neighbor's profit wherever I can or may . . . and labor faithfully that I may be able to relieve the needy."[59]

Willa Mae had become a Christian in prison. When she re-entered society, she had no material or financial resources. As she was part of our fellowship, ACTS paid her rent and provided her with a bus and train pass over a two-year period until she was able to sustain herself. Without this help, Willa Mae would have sunk deeper into financial poverty and poverty of the spirit.

The apostle Paul commands that we use our gifts for the benefit of others and God's honor and glory—because the gifts are His and on loan to us. 1 Corinthians 4:2 states, "It is required of stewards that they be found faithful." So, as faithful servants, deacons must assure that the available spiritual gifts and skills of the congregation are used wisely for the glory of God and the benefit of others.

Role #6: Deacons must be knowledgeable about local community resources.

How can community resources benefit church members and others? The government administers help massively, not individually. Deacons must see that municipal, state and federal governments are being good stewards of the Lord's resources by making them known. The prophet Haggai reminds us that these resources, also, belong to the Lord. Here, God states, "The silver is mine, and the gold is mine" (Hag. 2:8). Information about these resources needs to be communicated. How do we discover them? Not too many years ago, social service directories were printed and bound in large volumes to provide this information.

Now most municipalities and counties have online directories, as do other social service agencies. For instance, Greater Philadelphia United Way has www.211sepa.org, and in New Jersey there is www.nj211.org. The United Way agency has online lists in every state. Many municipalities also have a "211 hotline" to help people find services. There are many helpful religious-affiliated agencies. These ecumenical organizations, especially, exist to help people navigate a sometimes confusing social service system. I've found the Salvation Army, Lutheran, Episcopal, Catholic Social Services and Jewish Vocational Services extremely helpful. Knowledge of resources and resource personnel allows us to make good use of government, religious and private agency resources as we minister to people in word and deed. Knowledge of the best resources and lists of the same will benefit us and those we serve. At Tenth, we developed a list of the best public and private social services and Christian resources.

Role #7: Deacons must empower needy nonmembers to make good use of all available community resources and institutions of mercy.

I've heard many people say "I thought the church was supposed to help people"—meaning "You have to give me what I want." What we must do is avoid developing a relationship of dependency with those coming for help. One principle to follow I've mentioned before: "Don't work harder than the people coming for help." Let's help as we are able—according to carefully prepared guidelines—but we should also have a convenient one or two page list of community resources to refer people to for help. This is what we have done, after gleaning from those resource lists that others recommend and adding to it those we know and trust. With this list, if we can't help someone, we can honestly state, "We are not able to do that, but here is another church or agency that can." Allow the person to use a phone and provide a name and phone number for the person to call. If the need is legitimate, they will make the call. Ordinarily this step leads to other successful steps and leads to greater self-sufficiency.

Role #8: Deacons must cooperate with neighboring Bible-believing churches.

Don't duplicate a ministry if a nearby church already provides the service. Obtain information on what resources and ministries are available within your local community and beyond. Then partner with them for mutual care of the people in your neighborhood. Cooperation and communication will also prevent a major portion of scams from taking place.

Diaconal ministry stands at the heart of the gospel and its mission to the world. *Diakonia* is a total surrender of life for the benefit of others. The basis for Christian discipleship is not knowledge or power or wealth. The basis for being a disciple is service. The model for the disciples in their following of Christ is not the ruler, nor the scribe. The valid model is the person who serves (see Matt. 20:28; Mark 10:45; John 13:1–7).

The role of the deacon in mercy ministry is to model Christ while discipling and apprenticing others. It is not the deacon's job to do the entire ministry themselves. But it is their job to see that ministry gets done. A simple statement of the deacon's role is (1) to be an evangelical witness of word and deed in both worship and service and (2) to encourage and motivate others to use their gifts for the glory of God and the benefit of others.

Summary for equipping leaders and servant-leaders

In the previous list I've detailed the role of the deacon according to my years of experience. Another "quick list" to remember follows:

1. Admit you don't have to do every task—give up the "right" to do everything (free yourself and set others free).

   a. Make a list of tasks you alone must do.

   b. What tasks do you really enjoy doing but can allow others to perform?

   c. What tasks would you rather have others perform?

2. Prepare people for service (fix "broken bones").

3. Equip people for service (repair torn nets).

4. Encourage, cheerlead, model and apprentice.

   a. What tasks require your giving to others the most time and instruction? (How can it be simplified?)

   b. What tasks require little instruction?

   c. What tasks require no instruction?

5. Make it your job to give ministry away in the joy of serving.

6. Give people permission—reasons/excuses—to use their gifts.

7. Delegate to others. Delegation uses the gifts of others. It tells others that they are important and appreciated. It benefits the church's body life because more parts are actively involved. It frees you for priority action.

   a. Give them all they need to do the job.

   b. Give them ownership of the task.

   c. Trust them to accomplish the task.

   d. Encourage them to do the task.

   e. Back off.

   f. Intercede only if absolutely necessary.

   g. Use this as a learning experience.

   h. Risk their making mistakes.

   i. Ask for feedback and give appropriate kudos.

These instructions can help you serve in a smarter way and prepare you to serve in every situation.

10

Serving in Specific Situations

I met Lillian at one of the nursing homes where we serve. On that occasion I was there solely to observe my leaders. I wasn't going to preach. I was not going to sing. I was not going to play an instrument. My goal on that day was only to observe and encourage. As a matter of fact, I hadn't planned on doing anything but sit and, perhaps, hold a large-print Bible and a songbook for one of the residents. So I sat down next to Lillian who was waiting for the service to begin.

Lillian was one of the residents who attended in her wheelchair. She was in obvious discomfort when I sat beside her. She was all hunched over and moaning. Her fingers looked gnarled and her facial expression showed her anguish. It was an awkward situation for me. I felt useless and had no idea what to do except to cry out to God silently in prayer for Lillian. And so I did just that. Soon the worship leader began his sermon and Lillian continued in her anguish while I continued praying. After the sermon the worship leader said, "Let's sing 'Amazing Grace'" and as the pianist played the prelude, I saw a visible change in Lillian. She seemed to straighten up a bit as if her memory was being stirred. The grimace on her face began to vanish. We sang through the first verse and the worship leader said, "I can tell that you really enjoyed singing that verse. Let's sing the first verse again." The prelude began and the Holy Spirit prompted me to place my hand on Lillian's. She stopped moaning and seemed to be more focused. With my hand on hers, I whispered to her the words, "Amazing grace, how sweet the sound that saved a wretch like me."

Suddenly, almost miraculously, she sat almost ramrod straight and she began mouthing the words of "Amazing Grace." I looked at her face and the lines of pain had vanished. Her lips opened and she began to sing the hymn ever so quietly. It was as if God recalled to her mind the knowledge of her own salvation in Christ because of His amazing grace. It was such a transformation in her—and in me too. I hadn't done anything except show up. Yes, I offered a gentle touch and softly spoken words. But, God did the rest.

I learned so much about myself and thought a lot about Lillian afterward—mostly, that I didn't expect to feel so uncomfortable in that situation . . . anxious about how she would respond. Would she give a dirty look? What would she think? Would she judge me? Would she seem angry? And, then, how would I respond? Would I feel ashamed or embarrassed? This was about serving the Lord . . . it wasn't about me! But, in a way, it was about me and my fear—my risk—of not being appreciated or liked. It was about my discomfort in a unique situation.

Perhaps you experience fear or lack confidence in some ministry situations. Perhaps you don't want to come alongside some people because you lack knowledge about them or their condition or fear how they will respond. That sounds normal. Other deacons have told me they are afraid of the following:

1. Not doing the right thing

2. Feeling inadequate

3. Feeling that they are not doing enough

4. Being responsible for helping, but not knowing how

5. Battling selfishness (not wanting to serve)

6. Trying hard to please but failing (who must we please?)

7. Stepping out of their comfort zone

Most people step out of their comfort zone when in contact with those who are in great need—those who are vulnerable or on the edge or terminally ill, like these:

1. The person in a wheelchair

2. People who are different

3. Seniors

4. Hospital patients

5. Someone who is grieving the loss of a child

6. A single parent

Final Tips

Here are some additional hints that I hope will aid you in in your ministry to others.

Hospital visitation is an important part of caring, yet most people find hospital visitation uncomfortable. Here are some helpful tips:

1. Learn about the condition or illness before you visit.

2. Pray before your visit for a heart of compassion.

3. Wash your hands before entering the room.

4. If you arrive and the door is closed, ask at the nurse's station if it is okay to go in.

5. If the person is sleeping, ask the nurse whether she should be woken up or if you should just leave a note to visit another time. (Perhaps it is time for meds?)

6. Note any sign indicating that masks, gowns or gloves are needed during visit.

7. If the room is crowded with visitors, then come back another time.

8. Make the visit about fifteen minutes in length.

9. After you greet the patient, ask "May I stay for a short time?" Sit in a chair and position yourself where the patient can easily see you.

10. Start with a question such as "How are you doing today?" rather than "Are you still feeling sick?" It is best to ask questions that can't be answered "yes" or "no."

11. Listen more than you talk. Be understanding. Don't jump in with advice. Let the patient have some control.

12. The patient might still have very practical concerns such as child care, housekeeping and finances and needs to communicate these. But, be prepared for her to either avoid discussing them for fear of revealing too much or of opening up and pouring out too much information.

13. Ask if you can read Scripture. (Is there a special verse?)

14. Ask if you may pray. Then offer a brief prayer (three sentences) before you leave.

15. Help in practical things such as refilling the water pitcher, answering the telephone, asking a nurse to stop by.

16. Show respect for the nursing staff and doctors irrespec-

tive of what past experiences you might have had with hospital staff.

17. Do not touch or adjust any equipment. Do not second-guess a doctor, tell the patient that God will bring total healing, play down the care she is receiving, talk about gossip or bad news or delve into her personal life.

18. Wash your hands after leaving and pray.

How do you act when you meet someone who is "different-ly-abled"? What happens when you are with someone who needs a wheelchair, is blind or deaf?

1. Don't assume that a person with a disability, other than a hearing loss, can't hear. Often we respond to a person with a disability by talking louder.

2. Don't assume that people with speech, hearing or physical problems have cognitive problems as well. In other words, don't treat them as if they were less intelligent than you.

3. Don't apologize for not understanding their speech or say you understand their speech when you don't. Just ask, "Will you say that again?" Or "Run that by me again, please."

4. If the speech is difficult to comprehend, listen carefully for the subject of the conversation. Pick out nouns and listen for action words to help focus your understanding.

5. Respect the person by speaking directly to him and not through a companion or a family member.

6. As you learn someone's world, the communication problems will diminish. After a while, the comprehension level will increase and the friendship will grow.

When speaking, avoid the words cripple, crippled, deaf and dumb, slow, crazy, invalid, acts funny, afflicted with, a victim of and suffers from. Also, avoid saying the disabled, the retarded, the cerebral palsied, the paraplegic. Instead, say Jim has cerebral palsy, the child has autism, persons with disabilities or Anne has a vision problem. Say Fred uses a wheelchair rather than Fred is confined to a wheelchair; Joyce uses sign language instead of Joyce talks with her hands. When stating that a person does not have a disability, stay away from the word normal.

What about shaking hands?

1. The general rule is to share the same social courtesies with the person with a disability as with those without disabilities.

2. If the person uses a hook, has a missing right hand or whatever makes shaking hands awkward, extend your hand anyway. The person may use his left hand, touch your shoulder or do whatever he does when greeting others.

3. Ask the person what he wants you to do. For example, I have a friend whose paralysis starts at the shoulders. He asks me to put my hand on his shoulder where he has feeling so the greeting means that much more.

If you are with someone who uses a wheelchair . . .

1. Remember that the wheelchair is an extension of the person. Don't pay more attention to the chair than you would to eyeglasses or a hearing aid.

2. If your conversation is going to last for more than a few minutes, position yourself on eye level. Don't lean over in a patronizing manner, but sit down or kneel.

3. Don't lean on or hang on to the chair.

4. If the person needs help, ask the user's permission before pushing the chair.

5. Before you push, be sure the person is secure and the brake is off. If you aren't sure how, don't be afraid to ask.

6. If you are entering an elevator, back the chair in so that the person is not left facing the rear wall.

What about communicating with the person who is deaf?

1. If you don't have eye contact, get the person's attention by waving or tapping him on the shoulder.

2. Face the person to give him a good view of your face so he can possibly read your lips.

3. Remember, a hearing aid amplifies every sound, not just speech. Make the environment as quiet as possible. Do not speak louder unless requested.

4. If you can, use some basic signs.

If you are with someone who is blind . . .

1. Identify yourself and anyone with you. For example, "This is David Apple. George Brown is on my left."

2. It's okay to ask, "Did you see the game last night?"

3. If you move, inform the person either by continuing to talk as you move or by saying, "Excuse me, I'm moving to your left/right."

4. If providing assistance seems appropriate, ask if you may help. If the answer is no, don't get upset. But observe, again, if help really is needed and repeat your offer of help. If he says yes, offer your elbow and lead.

5. If you come to a narrow passage, move your elbow back. This movement will indicate to your friend that he should step behind you. Stopping before a step or curb will let your friend know a step or curb is ahead or you may say, "step" or "curb."

6. As you are walking, warn of any upcoming danger, such as a low ceiling, a break in the sidewalk or an obstacle in the path traveled.

7. If your friend has a service dog, don't pet it. Wait until the dog is not working and ask for permission.[60]

Strange encounters

When you encounter someone who is different, try to let your actions be natural and spontaneous. Dr. Dan Gottlieb is a psychologist who lost the use of his legs in an accident. He wrote this in a newspaper article:

What is your first instinct when you see someone who is disfigured, deformed or just plain different? To look away? To act without thinking?

Many years ago, waiting to meet a colleague, I was sitting in the lobby of Hahnemann Hospital, my briefcase on my lap, drinking a cup of coffee—when a woman in an obvious hurry walked by and put a dollar in my cup! She clearly didn't see a man in a wheelchair. She saw someone who was "different" and responded quickly.

I tell this story frequently because it teaches us so much about ourselves. Our brains are hardwired to react instantly to members of our species who don't look or behave the way they "should." When we encounter someone with a disfigured body or acting in ways that don't fit the expected norm, we feel distress.

It happens so fast that we don't even know what we're feeling. Our first instinct, however, is to find a way to diminish our distress. That's why, when I go into a restaurant, the hostess will often ask my companion, "Where would he like to sit?" The hostess makes eye contact with my companion in order to lessen the stress of facing someone who is "different."

Sometimes our reaction to the distress takes the form of anger or harsh judgment. Parents of children on the autism spectrum tell me that when their child becomes agitated in a public place, they frequently get critical looks or even patronizing comments. The reason: Affixing blame can help diminish distress caused by the unusual behavior of others. It makes their world feel more orderly.

So what can we do? Since stress is hardwired, allow yourself to simply experience the stressful feelings without trying to avoid them. Make eye contact if you can. I have always believed that if you look in someone's eyes, you can find their humanity—and in that process, you can learn more about your own. If that woman in Hahnemann's lobby had been able to look into my eyes, she would have seen a fellow human, a quadriplegic who in fact has a great deal in common with her.[61]

How do I help someone who is grieving the loss of a child?

While you might not feel empathy towards someone who has lost a child, because you have never lost a child yourself, you can express sympathy. Unfortunately, bereaved parents rely on their close friends, church officers and family for compassion and these people often say and do hurtful things. A little reflection on the suggestions on these pages might help you better prepare to show the compassion that is needed to parents in grief.

What do I need to know?

Bereaved parents can be parents who have lost children in utero, at birth, while an infant, while a youth or even as an adult. The age doesn't change things—children will always be sons and daughters of parents. If you've never lost a loved one, don't expect to automatically know what the bereaved parents' needs are. When you go to pay them a visit, leave your expectations and best advice at home.

People do show some similarities in their grief, but people also show great differences— even between married people. Respect the differences. Grief is best viewed as a lifelong journey. Grieving doesn't follow a schedule. Public mourning, because of culture and tradition, typically has expectations already established. But an individual's journey through grief occurs on that individual's time schedule. People can get stuck along the way—such as stuck in deep anger or depression. If you believe this has happened, you would be best to encourage them to seek more experienced help.

Don't compare or judge people on how they respond to their pain and grief. As long as they are not doing something dangerous or illegal or harmful, give them room to grieve.

How should I act?

1. Listen and listen and, when you are tired of listening, listen some more.

2. Don't lecture bereaved parents with Scripture readings.

3. Seek practical ways to ease their responsibilities in life so they have more freedom to grieve. This could be mowing the lawn, food shopping, cleaning, etc.

4. Ask them if they would like to talk about their child or look at photographs. The deceased child is very much "alive" to them and still a big part of their lives.

5. Remember them over time such as during the holidays and on the birth date of their deceased child. Don't forget they are on a journey that takes time.

6. Ask them questions directly, don't beat around the bush. Ask them if they want company today, if they would like to get out of the house and go shopping or if they would like to be alone, etc.

7. Encourage parents to express their grief in their own individual ways. Allow them to spend time individually with their friends or people they feel they can relate to—it's okay for them to express their grief separately, in the other's absence.

The first week after a loss is often a good time to take care of business. God has given us the emotion of shock. This numbness allows us to function and take care of business. Once this wears off, parents can collapse and go through periods where they simply cannot handle even daily routine.

Once the shock wears off, people often look for ways to start over or regain control of life. Encourage them to make significant decisions slowly. They might look at moving their home, adopting a child, changing jobs, divorce, etc. These are often desperate attempts to control life or push away the grief.

Watch out for when the parents are unable to take care of the routine responsibilities such as paying the bills and sorting the mail, responding to health insurance requests for information or going to work, etc. See if you can even help with some of these responsibilities if they are getting backlogged.

The goal of the journey through bereavement is not to leave grief behind—for the lost loved one will never disappear—but to become functional grievers.

How can I learn more?

Talk to a parent who has lost a child in a similar circumstance so that you can increase your sensitivity to the needs of the bereaved parents you desire to help.

There are also many books in the Christian and secular bookstores on grief. Simple books on grief that stick to counseling facts could provide the basics. For example, it is generally held that people go through a similar cycle (that includes such emotions as shock, anger and acceptance) as they journey through grief. Some books provide good advice and some are not so good on describing healthy bereavement. It is best to ask for recommendations from someone you trust or seek out a Christian support group that can provide a reading list.

How do I help someone who is a custodial single parent?

Remember, first, that you are ministering to a family. It helps to understand what single parents are going through in order to provide the individual care they need and will respond to in healthy ways.

What do I need to know?

Remember, your focus is on the needs of the parent and the child(ren). Suspend judgment. Leave behind your presuppositions, if any (visualize putting them in a backpack and leaving them outside on the front steps).

1. A single parent must be treated with respect and integrity.

2. A single parent has suffered loss—whether through death, desertion, separation or divorce. She or he will exhibit all the stages of grief: shock, anger, bargaining, acceptance and—hopefully—forgiveness.

3. There has been a break in their family structure.

4. The noncustodial parent may be inaccessible.

5. In most cases there is a sudden lack of financial support and a decline in financial security.

6. In most cases there is a noticeable decline in the support of friends, family and church.

7. The single parent faces chaos and change.

8. The single parent faces fear of the future and worry about today.

9. The single parent has great concern for the children's needs—how they deal with change, fear, abandonment, reactions of friends and family. Also, how they respond to visitation (normally), but especially, if there is a history of violence/abuse or drugs/pornography by the noncustodial parent.

How should I act? Helping the parent.

If you desire to be more sensitive in caring for a single parent or her or his child(ren), learn about the many physical, emotional, spiritual and financial changes that have occurred and the problems the parent is facing.

1. Be available to talk.

2. Listen.

3. Observe.

4. Give time.

5. Ask permission before sharing appropriate information or advice.

6. Give reassurance of your love and availability.

7. Encourage open communication.

8. Establish a trusting relationship with the single parent family. Open your heart and home, providing hospitality for the family on a regular basis.

9. Phone the single parent regularly (reassures that the single parent is not alone).

10. Provide child care to give the single parent a well-earned break.

11. Mobilize the church to care for home repairs, transportation, meals, counseling, etc.

How should I act? Helping the child.

Marital breakups are traumatic, and as children experience the sights and sounds (angry and/or violent), they experience pain, sorrow and even brokenness. Friends and relatives can help by becoming involved and developing a trusting relationship over time. Remember, their parents—people they trusted the most—have hurt them horribly. They need others they can turn to.

1. Spend quality time with each child.

2. Become an "adopted" aunt, uncle or grandparent.

3. Give reassurance that the separation/divorce/death is not the child(ren)'s fault.

4. Help equip the child(ren) to deal with conflict and stress.

5. Help the child(ren) grieve (give them permission).

6. Provide recreational opportunities for the children.

How do I help someone who is elderly?

Families need encouragement in caring for elderly members. It helps to understand what elderly people are going through in order to provide the individual care they need and will respond to in healthy ways.

What do I need to know?

1. There is no magic number that defines when someone has finally reached "old age."

2. Elderly people are very active in making decisions about their living environments and about their own lives.

3. Elderly people want to preserve their independence and self-respect. They are often more flexible and adaptable to change than we give them credit for.

4. Most elderly people have at least one chronic health problem that does not disable them.

5. Families, friends and neighbors are valuable to their care.

6. Elderly people are not usually senile or poor.

7. Elderly people enjoy a social life, but health problems can restrict mobility and social isolation can cause psychological frustrations.

8. Elderly people's intelligence has not diminished nor have they lost their ability to learn.

9. Because of changes they experience, elderly people can develop emotional problems such as fear, anxiety and anger. This can be observed in stubbornness, distrust, focusing on the past and other signs.

How should I act?

If you desire to be more sensitive in caring for an elderly person, learn about the changes that are taking place and the problems he or she could be facing:

1. Depression is a common disorder and can cause fatigue, insomnia, headaches and a lack of appetite.

2. Bodily changes make them more sensitive to the cold and less able to perspire (which can lead more easily to heat exhaustion).

3. Changes to joints and bones can result in a loss of muscle strength, aches and stiffness and an increase in accidents and fractures. Osteoporosis is where bones become more breakable and is more frequent in women. Arthritis is quite common and any or all joints can be affected.

4. They become more susceptible to infections such as pneumonia.

5. They show problems with balance, movement and coordination.

6. Their eyes become more sensitive to light and they have a harder time seeing in the dark. Cataracts and glaucoma are common. They experience drying of the eyes.

7. They lose some of their hearing ability, starting with high frequencies. This can cause communication problems or frustrations.

8. Their sense of smell is reduced, and they begin using more sugar and salt on foods to give the food flavor. Malnutrition, because of such problems as improperly fitting dentures and difficulty in preparing and enjoying meals, can occur. They can also experience a dry mouth.

9. They may show some level of memory loss because of dementia or Alzheimer's disease.

10. The longer a person lives the more likely it becomes that he or she will have to deal with some kind of cancer. Common cancers to watch for are lung, prostate, breast, large intestine, rectal, stomach and uterine.

11. Diabetes must also be checked by a doctor.

12. Heart diseases often manifest themselves more with age. High blood pressure is common among the elderly. They experience an increased threat of a stroke.

13. Sleeping disorders can also be common.

Here are some things you can suggest to provide for a safer home environment for an elderly person:

1. Check to make sure the flooring is not a problem such as loose tiles, rugs that slip, overly plush carpet and thresholds at doorways they can trip on.

2. Can the number of stairs they need to climb be reduced?

3. Can storage spaces, cabinets and shelves that are used for daily living be made more reachable?

4. Install handrails or bars.

5. Make sure the chairs, sofa and bed are easy to get into and out of.

6. Provide adequate lighting and avoid fluorescent lights.

7. Install redundant alarms that can be both heard and seen.

8. Reduce the use of gas appliances as their sense of smell is diminishing and no longer serves to help warn of dangerous conditions.

9. Make sure kitchen appliances and controls are easy to reach and hard to accidentally turn on.

How can I learn more?

1. Always encourage an elderly person to consult with and visit her primary care physician regularly.

2. Make sure that any home adjustments are done by quali-fied people.

3. Consult with a social worker or doctor who can put you in contact with local agencies, such as an agency on ag-ing, for assistance and advice that is already available.[62]

Remember, we serve an audience of One, the God of all comfort. We serve Him who knows our grief and carries our sorrows. When we offer hope in a nursing home, hospital or to those who are differently-abled, God helps us alleviate loneliness, misery and despair. When we practice hospitality, we entertain angels unaware. When we extend a welcome to strangers, they become guests and see Jesus Christ in us. This is mercy ministry: through the power of the Holy Spirit, coming alongside people in need and showing the compassion and love of Jesus.

11

Frequently Asked Questions

What is the best way to help when help is requested? Whom must churches help? And to whom should they deny help (knowing it is the right choice)? What about those situations requiring the wisdom of Solomon—when showing mercy and being merciful requires gut-wrenching decisions? What about con artists? People always ask me for help in how to deal with them—panhandlers, too. Several times a week, I receive calls from deacons and others asking, "What do I do in this situation?" or "I did such and such and am not sure it was wise." Here are some frequently asked questions along with my responses.

How do I set limits?

Sometimes our benevolence can set a precedent. After a local church's deacon paid a member's utility bill, a power company representative began sending people to his church for help. Immediately the church alerted the power company to the church's policy of only paying the bills of members, frequent worshipers and residents of the block. Setting a limit publicly was vital. But it was too late as word spread that the church paid people's power bills.

Years ago, when Tenth Church had a food pantry, it seemed like EVERYONE came for help. We discovered that the service we provided was redundant (there were other food pantries and clothing closets near us), and many who lined up for food assistance sold the food we gave to small grocery stores—even after we placed Tenth Church labels on the products. As there were abundant resources within two to three blocks, we closed our pantry and began referring people elsewhere. This allowed us to put our energy in ministries that were needed.

In long-term cases, how long do you help in situations where the husband won't work or is addicted or doesn't seem to cooperate?

This is a difficult issue and needs to be dealt with on a case-by-case basis. Mercy ministry with families is not easy. If you withhold assistance, everyone in the family suffers. Each decision has consequences that affect spouses and children. When deacons are dealing with single individuals, there are natural consequences to his or her actions that are less difficult to deal with. There are fewer ripple effects that hurt others.

In session twelve of his deacon training series, Tim Keller says that showing mercy is painful. "Give until the need is gone," he says about helping members, and regarding nonmembers, he says, "Give until it hurts." He goes on about how similar deaconing is to being a boxer: "Consider this: you are in the ring, wearing boxing shorts and gloves . . . if you don't want to get hit, get out of the ring, remove your boxing gloves, etc."[63]

There are those who agree and those who disagree with the above statements. That is why we need the power of the Holy Spirit and wisdom in our decision making.

What do you do if someone with a need comes to the church at night?

One or more people may come to the church at night—perhaps during choir practice or another activity—requesting food or other assistance. Be careful not to set bad precedents like giving money in order to get rid of them. That is usually the key, money. Don't submit to the tyranny of the urgent. The requester had all day to find help for food. You can say, "No one is available to help you at this time (after hours). Please return tomorrow during the day (they probably won't return)." A good idea is to have a printed list of local resources and give it. Say, "I'm sorry, we are not able to provide cash." Be assertive (but kind); the person will usually leave. Deacons and others should be trained to say, "No," when tough love is appropriate. It helps to work in tandem with another adult. When in doubt, provide a limited form of help. If the need is food, it doesn't hurt to have peanut butter, jelly and bread available for the evening (or another spread if someone has a peanut allergy—plus something gluten-free, too).

What do you do if the one requesting help lives far away?

One church received a phone request for rent from a stranger residing ten miles away. The caller said her rent was three months in arrears as her daughter took the rent money and gambled it away in the casinos. Think: Why is she calling a church so far away? Is it a "shotgun" approach (contacting every church until one shot hits the target)? If appropriate boundaries are already set, you can say you are not able to help nonmembers who live outside a carefully, but compassionately designed geographic area. Churches should have a well thought out and written policy of whom they will or will not help (members, attenders, local neighbors, distant neighbors and others out-of-town). Geographic boundaries can be marked off by zip code, north-south or east-west lines, municipality or natural limits (i.e. river to river). Don't be afraid to say to such a requester, "We are not able to help, but here is the name and number of a church near you that might" (perhaps one that your church has fellowship with). You may also direct them to an online directory of social services or direct people to their local food pantries or clothing closets. (For more information, see Appendix B: Guidelines for Deacons.)

How many times do you feel you have been "taken advantage of" by those you sought to serve? How do you stay faithful during those times?

The longer people work with manipulative people the wiser they become. Experience has been a good teacher. I've been taken by the best con artists and I've learned a great deal. The most valuable lesson I've learned is that I don't need to please other people (especially those demanding help). I serve an audience of One (Jesus). Seeking after obedience and a right relationship with God keeps me trusting, praying fervently and able to serve others well.

How do you respond when someone seeking help also asks you for a ride home?

The first thing to consider is your own safety. Do you know this person? If the person is a complete stranger and you know nothing about him or her, then you are placing yourself in a dangerous situation. You do not know, and cannot control, what will occur once you are in the car together. We have rules to protect our volunteer staff that says not to provide rides, not to give money and not to give personal contact information. A wise response in this case is, "I'm sorry, I am not able to do that."

How do you put mercy into practice? What is your philosophy?

I have four simple principles (plus using common sense): Be available, get involved (that is, come alongside to help someone in need), establish relationships and offer hope. Ministry is really "just showing up" and letting God work through you. Seek to be faithful servants of our Lord. Seek to follow Jesus model of coming alongside people for a while (see John 1:14), visiting widows and orphans (see James 1:27) and helping the least of these (see Matt. 25:31–46).

How do you figure out who is deserving of help?

None of us is deserving. Scripture says that while we were God's enemies, Christ died for us (see Rom. 5:7–10). Praise God that Jesus drank the cup of wrath in our place so we could drink the cup of salvation. God is a God of grace, and ministry is about mercy and grace—loving the unworthy and the unlovely. We befriended a cross-dresser (a man who dressed as a woman) and this guest attended one of our Bible studies. The first time that "she" came to the Bible study, I was standing at the church door to offer a welcome. When she entered, I shook her hand, welcomed her and then saw that she was really a guy. I felt repulsed and thought to myself, "I don't want this person in here. This is a holy place." Immediately God convicted me of my judging her. Who else besides sinners should we want to study the Word with us? We don't have the power to change this person or others, but God can do the changing as we make ourselves available to be used by Him in mercy ministry (1:16).

If someone asks me for money on the street, what should I do?

Never give cash. Instead, try to make it a win-win situation. If someone says he or she is hungry, invite the person to join you for a meal (in a public place, never your home). Share your lunch in a park if possible. Scripture encourages help in kind, not in cash (see James 2:15-16; Rom. 12:20). If the person requesting help really wants food and not cash he or she will take you up on the offer. The best way to help is to establish a relationship. But, don't be afraid to say "no" if the person continues to want cash and your offer of food is rejected. Say, "I'm sorry, I'm not able to do that." Once, while walking to my office someone walked beside me and said, "Can you help me get something to eat?" I offered my lunch; he said he had food allergies. I offered to buy him something at the corner market; he said they didn't have anything he could eat. I said, "I guess I can't help you!" He walked away.

I also have in my office a microwave oven and microwavable meals. I encourage people who request food to meet with me and talk.

If someone comes to the church asking for money, what do I do?

Our policy is never give cash, only gifts in kind. We provide valuable agency referrals to those seeking help. Since 1988 we've concluded that at least 95 percent of those asking for help are con artists who don't need the "help" they are requesting, but want cash. Don't be afraid to say you can't help. People who are looking for fast cash actually appreciate a "no" answer and will leave. They don't want to waste their time if the answer is no!

We will help those who are members, regular attenders and those who are closely associated with our outreach ministries. With those, we seek to say YES to their requests as we are able.

Are there "red flags" (warning signs) I should be aware of?

In many cases "well-meaning people" are drawn to the tyranny of the urgent. This is a lethal form of manipulation that causes us to fall into the trap of con artists and others. One person said his mother had died the week before and that he had spent all his available money on the funeral. He said he had no money for food. The man again asked for cash, and when I refused, he berated me for not trusting him, claiming to be a pastor with twenty years of experience.

What about people who claim to be from out of state and are "stranded"?

Be wary of these requests which are just as lethal as email solicitations for help. I received the following phone call. I quote the conversation word for word. "Thank you for taking my call. The Philadelphia Presbytery office referred me to you for help. My name is Michael and I live in California. I'm attending a funeral in Philly and—well, I ran out of money and my credit cards are maxed out. I need $86 to pay my hotel bill or they will evict me. I have nowhere else to stay or store my twelve pieces of luggage. I can't get in a shelter. I called all the shelters including [here he names one] and they can't help me. Can you help me? Listen, I'm using a borrowed phone which I have to return in just three minutes. What do you say? Will you help me? It is the end of a business day and no one can help me. It seems that no one wants to help a Christian."

This con is one of my all-time favorites. How many different "red flags" do you see here? First, the caller says he was referred by the Philadelphia Presbytery. This is the office of the mainline denomination, not the PCA, Tenth's denomination. They would refer people to the local PC-USA church (there is one two blocks away) or other churches with whom they have regular contact. We have had no business dealings with this office. Next, this is a manipulation story in that he needs help immediately. There is the matter of all that luggage. How many people need twelve pieces of luggage to attend any event, much less a funeral? Of course, he is using a borrowed phone and—here he is trying to put the pressure on me—"I have three minutes to make a decision." One more time he applies pressure, saying that it's the end of the business day meaning there is not much time left for him to get help. And then he plays his "trump card" that no one wants to help a Christian, meaning our church must help him because he says that.

What experience has impacted you the most?

In 1988, soon after I began ministering at Tenth, I hosted a table at our Community Dinner (a banquet for our homeless neighbors). I believed wrongly that because of my urban ministry experience I could facilitate a conversation at my table without any difficulty. So, to begin, I asked Horace, one of the men at my table, "Who is your hero?" He looked around the room at 120 others and said loudly, "Look at them. Do you know what I see? Losers, nothing but losers. We don't have any heroes, so don't even talk to me about heroes." At that point I felt very small, inadequate and ashamed. As I was going to reply, another said, "Do you know what? Not only are we losers, we are all no good, rotten bastards." I didn't know what to say next. My inclination was to sink under the table or disappear entirely. As I recall, I changed the subject and began talking about football. In reflection, I learned a lot from that experience: my table guests described the way everyone is in their unsaved condition. But, when we come to salvation in Christ we are no longer losers or no good or rotten or bastards. We become worthy. Though our sins are like scarlet (see Isa. 1:18) and our righteous acts as filthy rags (see 64:6), in Christ's righteousness we are heirs, children of our victorious, almighty God.

Additional Questions

We live in an affluent, suburban community. There are certainly needs around us like broken families, spousal abuse, addiction, juvenile delinquency. Is it acceptable to stay in our environment showing mercy, or does God call us to step outside and meet the needs of the poor/oppressed? And how do we do that in a way that is organic and not scripted by a formal program?

I believe the crucial aspect here is that God calls us according to our gifts. I like to paraphrase a couple of Bible passages for my own use, "God has given you gifts. Use them" (see Rom. 12:3-8), and "When you have opportunity to do good, do it" (see Prov. 3:27-28). Ministry requires being in relationship. God calls some "to step outside the affluent community" to minister elsewhere, but not others. In every community, there is hidden and visible economic poverty plus poverty of spirit and oppression, brokenness and brokenheartedness. This is the darkness into which we are all called to be light. Some are called sooner than others, some later, according to God's timetable. We must, over time, find the courage to enter into the hard, parched ground of our own heart and ask Him to change it into a well-watered garden. Then we can serve wherever God has planted us—whether in a city, suburb or rural area.

How can someone who has "grown up Christian" minister to those who live such sordid lives? How can middle/upper-class Christians relate better to those who are extremely different from them?

I believe what I am hearing is "How can someone like me minister to sinners like them?" So much has to do with our relationship with Christ. A colleague who worked alongside me in homeless outreach once said, "I am just one beggar telling another beggar where to find bread." I believe that people are all pretty much the same across economic, cultural and ethnic lines. We all have the same need for repentance and to develop a healthy relationship with God and neighbor. I believe if we think of ourselves as different or better than others, we deceive ourselves and cannot serve God at all.

Can you suggest practical ways we can be welcoming, loving & less intimidating to people who are different than us?

Practically speaking, I believe the late Catholic theologian Henri Nouwen had it right when he said turn your hostility into hospitality. By doing so, we turn strangers into guests and act as loving hosts to them. Nouwen describes each person as a gift that we have the privilege of unwrapping.[64]

Most of our outreach ministries involve coming to the table together. It is very simple. We sit, eat and talk. We are welcoming. We provide hospitality. We establish relationships and trust. We make the church a safe place for everyone.

Within the mercy ministries, do you always try to meet the spiritual need in addition to the physical? Or, do you have some ministries that only seek to meet the physical need?

We always try to offer an alternative to what the world is providing. For instance, a homeless shelter may offer a feeding program. They provide for a physical need. People generally eat quickly and don't stay long enough to establish any relationships. Our goal in ministry is primarily to feed the spiritual bread and establish relationships. We believe that without sharing the gospel of Jesus Christ, there is no mercy. We need to provide evidence that we are different from secular programs.

How do we integrate people of varied backgrounds (i.e., poor or homeless) into the culture of the church so they feel comfortable and at home?

A lot depends on whether the "culture" of the church is welcoming or hostile to such strangers. One measure of a caring culture is how the church treats its own members who are on the fringe and loosely connected. Are some stigmatized or ignored because they are different? Are some deemed less worthy and treated less equally because of certain disabilities or characteristics? Small groups are a great way to provide hospitality, relationships and encouragement to those who newly arrive at the doors of your church.

Do you have people from the street (homeless people) attending Sunday worship at Tenth Presbyterian Church and feeling at home?

Tenth welcomes everyone who wishes to enter the church to worship. Most of our homeless neighbors enter the church initially through the "side door"—Fellowship Bible Study and Community Dinner ministries. There they establish relationships with Tenth members who provide easier access to corporate worship. This is true for other bridge-building ministries as well—such as Tenth International Fellowship, for example.

If you were at our suburban church, how would you begin to stir us toward these urban ministries and concern for the poor?

At every church where I am invited to speak or teach, my goal is to open up the Scriptures and share God's heart for the broken and brokenhearted. I do this by praying that God will change people's hearts. I know that I cannot change anyone. All I can do is share the truth and my excitement for ministry. Transformation comes solely through the power of the Holy Spirit. There are people in every congregation who have listening ears and are attuned to God's message. By reading the Word, listening to messages about mercy and compassion ministries and reading books about urban missions, God raises up and stirs up people for this work.

My life is completely insulated from inconvenience and contact with the poor and needy. How can I repent and start to reach out? Where do we begin? Where did you begin?

Repentance, as I understand it, is a complete turnaround of attitude and lifestyle. It is a spiritual movement from self-reliance to total dependency on Christ and acknowledges that we are spiritually bankrupt. When you or I realize that we are nothing, and salvation is based not on who we are or what we have accomplished, but is solely the work of Christ, we begin to see things differently. If prior to this, it was "inconvenient" for us to have contact with the poor, now we should see others as a brother or sister. A Jewish proverb speaks of this:

> An elderly rabbi once asked his pupils how they could tell when the night had ended and the day had begun. "Could it be," asked one of the students, "when you see an animal in the distance and can tell whether it's a sheep or a dog?" "No," answered the rabbi. Another asked, "Is it when you can look at a tree in the distance and tell whether it is a fig tree or a peach tree?" "No," said the rabbi. "Then when is it?" the pupils demanded. "It is when you can look on the face of a man or woman and see that it is your sister or brother. Because. . . if you cannot see this, it is still night."[65]

If you moved to serve in another region, what would you do first?

I would initially want to meet area pastors and leaders and discover what resources were available or lacking in the churches and community. I would assess public and private agencies to determine how well they function and how much they are appreciated by the local community. I would determine which churches held to the inerrant teaching of Scripture and how their congregations live this out in their neighborhoods and cities. In addition, I would want to find out who are the "gatekeepers"—the most important leaders in the community, long-time merchants, neighborhood historians, etc.

How do you minimize risks in ministry?

In normal human relationships there are occasions when we are mistreated, misrepresented, rejected and persecuted. This occurs as much, if not more, in ministry situations. I believe the biggest risk or fear we face in ministry is not being able to meet our own expectations. We so much want to please people whom God has brought to us. Many times we are afraid they won't like us or appreciate the service we provide. But this is an unbiblical response. Our goal, biblically, is to glorify God by doing our best in all things (see 1 Cor. 10:31). In addition, ministry tasks should have clear descriptions, and guidelines should be clearly understood about where our responsibilities end in assisting others.

What is the motive for service and mercy?

As a follow-up to the above (minimizing risks), we should serve out of gratitude to God for our salvation. Our entire life should be lived out as a sacrifice of thanksgiving. I am reminded that the French word *merci* means thank you. A further glance in the dictionary indicates the word's origin comes from a mercantile or business exchange. How can we not live out our lives as a thank you to God for buying us out of the slave market of sin and giving us eternal life?

Would you send volunteers from your church to an agency serving the community that is affiliated with another denomination?

It is vital that we establish relationships with these social service providers. This is the basis or foundation for developing partnerships with their "gatekeepers" (people who can show us the way to helpful resources). Of course, it is equally important to be circumspect and to use wisdom and discernment when doing so. While I would discourage cooperating with an Islamic mosque; a Baha'i, Buddhist or Krishna temple; Jehovah's Witnesses or Mormons, we can agree on the "nonnegotiables" of

Scripture with most Roman Catholics, evangelicals, Seventh Day Adventists and mainline Protestant denominations. Our volunteers represent Jesus Christ when they serve, and we are His "sent ones" in the world. I've worked with institutions where the volunteer director or chaplain is Muslim or a cult member or a nominal Christian. What they respect and appreciate the most are good, consistent and faithful volunteers. The bottom line is that we glorify God and benefit those we seek to serve. So, my answer is a simple YES. Let's saturate our communities with incarnational Christians who will proclaim the gospel in both word and deed.

How did you start your ministry? What were your first steps?

The ministry started in 1983 when a Bible study group saw a homeless person sleeping on the church steps. They approached the deacons with the need and the deacons replied, "What do you want to do?" This empowered them to pray and take small successful steps. What began as the vision of a small group has grown to several ministries with over two hundred fifty volunteer staff. Our ministry has also become an urban laboratory for nurturing future servants and developing ministries elsewhere.

How do you recruit volunteers for your ministry?

We communicate to the congregation via e-mail, blogging, bulletin announcements, pulpit talks and posters. We also have a volunteer link on our websites activecompassionphilly.org and tenth.org. The best way, however, is face to face. I share a task and make it convenient, specific and measurable. I then ask people to pray about participating. This way their yes or no answer is not to please me, but to honor God.

How have you partnered with other people/organizations in the area to meet local needs?

We invite other Bible-teaching churches to work with us regularly, and I am available to train their members and their deacons. Many members of the community volunteer and work side by side with our Christian staff. I also open up my diaconal and mercy training to over one hundred churches in and around Philadelphia.

What kind of leadership structure do you have in place?

We have developed leadership teams for all our ministries. These teams are accountable to each ministry's coordinator who has been empowered to carry out all the tasks of their ministry. They, in turn, are accountable to me. I do not interfere or micro-manage them unless I am aware of sinful or harmful behavior. I am accountable to Tenth's executive minister.

How do you decide which types of ministries you offer?

We focus on the needs in our neighborhood and the needs someone may bring to our door. Also important is what our members are passionate about. Thus we have ministries to home-less persons, incarcerated men and women (adult and juvenile), nursing home residents, separated and divorced, single parents and children whose parent(s) are incarcerated. Our church has also developed ministries to those with sexual struggles, people with AIDS and those seeking alternatives to abortions. These last three have grown to be incorporated as their own 501(c)3 religious nonprofit organizations.

What are some of your greatest failures/successes?

Since 1988, God has provided many learning experiences and occasions where I've been severely stretched. I can't say there have been failures. Each experience has allowed me to grow in Christian maturity and trust in God who keeps drawing me to the foot of the cross for confession and repentance. As I have a natural, selfish desire to do things my own way, I struggle daily to become totally dependent upon God and to trust Him for everything. I have seen much fruit in the salvation of the lost, attitude changes among elders, deacons and others leaders (myself included), the provision of seminars and conferences, seminary teaching and church consultations.

What advice would you give? What are your "lessons learned"?

Remember that God is in charge. He is sovereign over the timetable and the fruit of ministry. While I am thoroughly delighted to see God working in the lives of people, I have learned to trust God for the outcome and find joy in obedient service. I believe it is important to move slowly by surrendering our desire to want quick results. I've learned to seek to please God only and not people (with the principle that we serve *an audience of One*). I view myself as expendable and that my role is to equip, empower and mobilize the church and to cooperate with others in the faith.

Have you gotten requests from travelers?

On two occasions I received similar requests for help from women appearing or claiming to be pregnant. The story has this woman and her husband driving south on Interstate 95 when their car breaks down. They are from Boston. On one occasion the woman came to the church, and on the other a different woman telephoned. Each request was the same: they are from out of town, their car broke down on the highway, they don't know anyone in Philly and they need this specific auto repair part which costs seventy-five dollars. They are desperate. They need your help.

What would you do? Would you help them? How would you handle it? First, consider the facts. They live in a distant city. They have no relatives or friends in Philadelphia. And where they indicate their car broke down is five to six miles away from our church. How did they know to contact Tenth or come directly to our Delancey Street office? How did they know to call us for help?

How do I help my adult son?

I received this call: "*My adult son is currently at the detention center awaiting an arrest hearing. He is already on probation. I know he'll probably serve some time, but sooner or later will be released. In the past we allowed him to move in with us, setting down house rules and boundaries which he did not keep. He got drunk the first night and two more times. We ended up finding and paying for his apartment. He worked, but he spent his pay on alcohol and drugs and did not pay his rent and utility bills.   My fear is that he will want to live with us once he is released. He has anger issues and can become physically abusive when he's high or drunk. He is destroying my husband and me, and we don't want him to live here again. Yet, we also feel guilty about turning him away. When does Christian charity turn into enabling and placing us into another unsafe situation?   We don't need any further drama at this point.*"

My answer: "I grieve for you and your husband. What you write about your son's actions is not unexpected. His actions—

lying, deception, manipulation and conniving—will not stop. It is the common behavior of someone with a chemical addiction. You can't change him, but you can change how you (and your husband) respond to his requests. I believe that submitting to his desire to return to your home will only permit him to sin more and more against you, and this is a pattern that has been repeated over and over again.

You have a situation where saying YES to him will only cause more pain and will not help. Saying NO now (and in the future) is the most loving thing you, as a parent of an adult child, can do. It will also be a God-honoring decision as you are disciplining a son (as God disciplines sons)—not to harm, but to encourage maturity and growth. Your son is crying out for help. You can help him by not giving in to his pleas and demands. There are real Christ-centered solutions for long-term recovery and accountability which will not encourage greater dependency, plus boundaries that need to be set. We can speak about these if you'd like. Remember that boundaries keep you safe and protected only as long as you keep the gate closed and locked."

How do we put service into practice? How do I love this person at this time?

Prayer is vital for mercy ministry. There needs to be a balance between what I want to do and what I believe God is doing and will do. I was working with one person for several months helping him with transportation needs and also providing spiritual counsel. One day he called me from jail asking for bail money. "What should I do?" I asked myself. I wanted to bail him out, and at the same time, wondered if that was a right decision. I did not want to develop another dependency. If I refused, my guest would spend sixty days in jail. Could God work in that situation? Knowing the answer, I refused, but ministered to him in jail.

What do you think about my inviting homeless persons to my home?

In general, our policy is to meet with homeless guests at church, a restaurant or other public place. For safety reasons, we advise people not to invite them to homes, provide home addresses and phone numbers or to give rides in a car. It is a good idea to do things as a group and not alone. Of course, as our guests show fruit of growth in Christ and life changes, we relax the rules accordingly. But safety must come first.

Conclusion

I began this book sharing a story of life and death and how the Bible is the story of eternal redemption—how God takes the trauma and brokenness of His redeemed and transforms them into gifts for His use in ministry. I have sought to share why I do mercy ministry, how ACTS Ministries and Tenth Presbyterian Church provide mercy ministry and how you, too, can show the love of Christ in mercy ministry. I hope that the stories and the reproducible ministry models I've shared will be of great benefit to you, your churches and your communities. *Soli deo gloria.* To God be the glory. Great things He has done.

Appendix A: Resources

Here are several resources that I recommend.

Web

ACTS: Active Compassion Through Service
www.activecompassionphilly.org

Biblical Guidelines for Mercy Ministry in the PCA
www.pcahistory.org/pca/2-414.html

Christian Community Development Association.
www.ccda.org

CRC Canada Mercy Ministries
www.diaconalministries.com

Faith & Service Technical Education Network
www.fastennetwork.org/

Mission to North America
www.pcamna.org

Tenth Presbyterian Church
www.tenth.org

Print resources

Steve Corbett and Brian Fikkert: *When Helping Hurts*

Gerard Berghoef and Lester DeKoster: *The Deacons Handbook*

Timothy J. Keller: *Ministries of Mercy*

Timothy J. Keller: *Resources for Deacons*

Bobert D. Lupton: *Toxic Charity*

Ronald J. Sider, Philip N. Olson & Heidi Rolland Unruh: *Churches That Make a Difference* (featuring Tenth and others)

Amy L. Sherman: *Restorers of Hope*

Alexander Strauch: *The New Testament Deacon*

Jay Van Groningen: *Changing Times, New Approaches: A Handbook for Deacons*

Lori Wiersma and Connie Kuiper VanDyke: *The Deacon's Handbook*

Appendix B: Guidelines for Deacons

The following guideline was created by a former minister in the Germantown section of Philadelphia. I include it here so many will not need to reinvent the wheel.

Guidelines for Deacons

Purpose

Our purpose is to provide spiritual counseling and material assistance in the Name and to the glory of Jesus Christ. Our intention is to keep this ministry as an explicit testimony to the love of Jesus Christ, not simply to provide services.

Scope

This ministry is designed to reach 1) Christians within our church, 2) Christians outside our church and 3) those who are not Christians (Gal. 6:10; John 17:20–21). We intend to supplement existing channels of help, rather than to replace them, since every good source of help has God as the origin (James 1:16–17). Help will take the forms of financial and spiritual counseling and/or material aid. Financial problems usually have a spiritual origin. We will try to present the gospel and to give Christian literature to the unsaved and to use biblical principles to direct both the unsaved and the saved to our Lord. We will encourage and invite those who do not have a church home to worship with us.

Exclusions

1. We cannot help nonmembers who live outside a carefully, but compassionately designed geographic area. We have determined who we will help and not help (members, attenders, local neighbors, distant neighbors, others out-of-town). These boundaries are marked off by zip code, north-south or east-west lines, municipality or natural limits (i.e. river to river). You might say to such a requester "We are not able to help, but here is the name of a church that might (one that you are in fellowship with)." You may also provide a list of community services or direct people to local food pantries or clothing closets.

2. We cannot assist any person who appears to be under the influence of alcohol or other drugs and those whose behavior is belligerent.

Long-term benevolence

Long-term benevolence is a case with regular, reasonably identifiable debts which continue into the future. Generally, a budget is required and its plan will be for a period of no longer than twelve months. When appropriate, cases must be taken through the reapproval process. Accountability is an important part of long-term benevolence. An elder would be assigned to work with the deacons and would include conditions such as financial counseling, minimum job hunting efforts or other reasonable requirements.

Administration

1. Since deacons were given responsibility to administer distribution to the widows in Acts 6:1–3, this is a legitimate expression of their office. We recommend that at least four be selected (including at least one deaconess, if the church has this office) with the following gifts represented: mercy, helps, administration. The Benevolence Ministry Director, upon the approval of one other ministry member, will contact the church treasurer to disburse funds from the Benevolence Ministry account. Periodic reports of the work of the ministry will be submitted to the deacon board and forwarded to the elders.

2. Record keeping is consistent with good stewardship, but nothing will be done to intentionally humiliate applicants or recipients of assistance. However, prudence and experience indicate that cash should not be given to recipients, but to those providing goods and services. Transients may be referred, upon approval, to a local gas station/motel/restaurant with which the church has an arrangement to pay, for a specific number of meals/nights of lodging/amount of gas.

3. A periodic review of the recipient's situation, in the case of short-term and long-term help, will be done by a debt/budget counselor to see if the same needs exist. This budget counseling is required in order to give more than superficial care. Those trained within the church (not necessarily deacons) will be asked first to counsel,

but other trained counselors will be contacted in case of need. If financial counsel is ignored or rejected, assistance will be terminated.

4. Assistance will stop when the need is met, when a suitable job has been refused or when deemed advisable by the Benevolence Ministry.

Screening

1. A genuine need must exist, as determined by the Benevolence Ministry, using whatever information is needed for an accurate judgment. This includes an interview and completion of an information form.

2. Transients are a distinct kind of applicant, since some seek to make a living by defrauding churches. The name of the transient will be checked against any available community database, and at least one valid telephone number of someone known to the transient will be called to verify the identity and possibly the need of the applicant. Some transients claim to be hungry, but want cash and will not go to a restaurant. Pressure may be applied, but wisdom dictates that some kind of background check be made. We do not give cash, but gifts-in-kind only, such as food coupons, store vouchers or gift certificates.

3. Widows are a special concern of the church. 1 Timothy 5:3–16 clearly gives the qualifications for a widow to be helped by the church. Among them, children and grandchildren are to bear the responsibility to help the widow, and the church should intervene if that assistance

does not and will not exist. The wisdom of the Spirit is needed in many instances when assisting single mothers who are not widows. We want to show the love of Christ in every situation.

4. When a person can work, even part-time, this is required by Scripture (2 Thess. 3:10). For example, if a doctor indicates that a person can work, it would be expected, and this work gives a greater sense of dignity.

Funding

Funds designated by individuals, by the church or by other sources for Benevolence Ministry shall comprise the funds available. No money will be borrowed to continue giving help, nor promises made for ongoing help without a certain assurance of funds being available. If funds are exhausted, the church assumes no liability to continue giving aid (2 Cor. 9:8–12).

Networking

James 1:16–17 shows that all good gifts come from the Father. A ruler is called "God's servant to do you good" (Romans 13:4, NIV 1984). Therefore, from whatever source help is obtained, it is legitimate, except when the testimony of the church is compromised. All funds belong to God (Hag. 2:8; Ps. 50:10–11). The ministry may request help from community services and provide help at their request and our approval.

Training

Since trained Christian financial counselors are crucial in situations of ongoing assistance, the Benevolence Ministry will try to recruit them and may provide for the costs involved in training.

Crown Financial Ministries has a Counselor Self-Study Course that can be pursued at home at modest cost. These materials can be obtained at www.crown.org or at 800-722-1976.

Procedures

1. If contact is made through the church office during working hours, the secretary will obtain the name of the applicant, where and how communication can be made with them, the general nature of the need and whether or not this person has contacted our church before.

2. The secretary will convey the information to a member of the ministry and will contact a second member to be assigned to the need.

3. The ministry members assigned will communicate with the applicant, either in person or by phone, to get a brief history and picture of needs, using the information sheet when possible. The history and need should be somehow verified, possibly by contacting a relative or friend of the applicant. Some will seek to receive dishonest gain from the church.

4. If the person is a transient, they should be contacted after verifying some aspect of their need. If the applicant lives locally, a trained counselor should determine the needs and underlying causes, make a proposal to the ministry and arrange to see the recipient, normally once a month.

5. If contact is made outside of normal working hours, or if no secretary is available, any ministry member may make the initial contact and, with another available adult (never alone), conduct the interview.

General guidelines

1. Present the gospel, including giving a good tract and paperback Bible. The gospel is the best solution for the needs of the unsaved, since it will have positive economic consequences.

2. Verify needs and some history. Ask for references and call them, even if only a one-time request. Contact a community-screening agency, if available.

3. More than $_____ will not be expended on one participant (or family) without Deacon Board approval.

4. No cash should be given directly to applicants.

5. Do not visit an applicant alone. Interview the applicant with another ministry member, both for protection from possible charges and because one will often discern issues that the other missed. The initial interview team should have at least one male and, if the applicant is a woman or a family, one female.

6. Give the recipient the opportunity to earn a contribution, perhaps by helping around the church, if there is not a security issue.

7. Require a degree of responsibility for those who receive ongoing assistance, such as following a budget. They should be responsible to a budget counselor.

8. Keep records and information confidential, except with those who need to know, with the consent of the applicant, and keep the records in a locked file at the church. If the applicant does not consent to have pertinent information shared as necessary, then they will not be helped.

9. Assistance should not be given without the agreement of one other member of the ministry.

10. Try to work with the applicant's home church, if this pertains, and try to encourage them to attend a church, if this does not.

11. Pray for discernment and wisdom, preferably with the applicant present.[66]

Appendix C: Sample Talent Survey

SAMPLE TALENT SURVEY – THERE ARE MANY NEEDS IN THE BODY OF CHRIST, AND WE ARE HOPING TO BEGIN TO MEET THEM THROUGH YOUR STEWARDSHIP. PLEASE INDICATE BELOW HOW YOU WOULD LIKE TO SERVE OUR LORD AS OPPORTUNITIES ARISE.

I WOULD LIKE TO MINISTER TO:
____ PEOPLE WITH AIDS
____ HOMELESS
____ SENIORS
____ SHUT-INS
____ SINGLE PARENTS
____ WIDOWS/WIDOWERS
____ CHILDREN
____ PHYSICALLY DISABLED
____ DEVELOPMENTALLY DISABLED

I AM AVAILABLE:
____ DAYS FROM _____ TO _____
____ EVENINGS FROM_____TO _____
____ WEEKDAYS
____ WEEKENDS
____ DAILY
____ ONCE PER WEEK
____ ONCE PER MONTH
____ OTHER _____

I WILL HELP WITH:
____ACCOUNTING/FINANCIAL ADVICE
____ART/GRAPHIC DESIGN
____AUTO MAINTENANCE/REPAIR
____BUDGETING
____CARPENTRY REPAIR
____CHILD CARE (FOR AGES _____)
____PHONE CALLS
____ROOFING REPAIRS
____RUN ERRANDS (DRIVING)
____SECURITY DURING WORSHIP
   SERVICE
____COUNSELING
____DISH WASHING

____PERSONAL GROOMING/HYGIENE
____PHOTOGRAPHY
____PLUMBING/HEATING REPAIRS
____PRAYER
____READING
____REASSURANCE
____CLEANING/HOUSEWORK
____COMPUTER
____COOKING (INDIVIDUALS)
____COOKING (LARGE GROUP)
____SEWING/DRESSMAKING
____SHOPPING
____SITTING WITH SHUT-INS

____ELECTRICAL/APPLIANCE REPAIR	____SOLDERING/WELDING
____HAIR CUTTING	____TAX PREPARATION
____HAULING – HAVE VAN/TRUCK	____TILE WORK
____HEALTH CARE	____TUTORING (3Rs / ESL)
____HOSPITALITY – MEALS	____TYPING/CLERICAL
____HOSPITALITY – OVERNIGHT	____UPHOLSTERY
GUESTS	____LAUNDRY/IRONING
____USHERING DURING WORSHIP	____LEGAL
SERVICE	____VISITATION
____LOCK INSTALL/REPAIR	____WINDOW WASHING
____MAILING/FOLDING/INSERTING	____WORD PROCESSING
____MUSIC (VOCAL/INSTRUMENTAL)	____WRITING/CORRESPONDENCE
____PAINTING/WALLPAPERING	____ OTHER _____

VOCATION _____

HOBBY _____

Name _____

Home Phone _____

Adress _____

E-mail _____

If there is an emergency need I will give blood. My blood type is _____

Appendix D: Servant Leaders

The following excerpt is from the book, *Servant Leaders*, by Ben Vandezande which is out of print and no longer available. I believe it is valuable enough to be included in this book.

The visiting deacon: coming alongside those in need

As an ordained servant, God has called you to serve in a ministry of mercy and compassion. The God who called will also equip you to do your calling. Therefore minister to poor and rich alike. Be compassionate to the needy. Encourage them with words that create hope in their hearts and with deeds that bring joy to their lives. Let your lives be above reproach; live as examples of Christ Jesus; look to the interests of others

Visiting

Visiting people is the heart of the deacon's work. Deacons visit as representatives of God, the "Father of our Lord Jesus Christ, the Father of compassion and the God of all comfort, who comforts us in all our troubles, so that we can comfort those in any trouble with the comfort we ourselves have received" (2 Cor. 1:3–4, NIV 1984). You serve as a channel of Christ's love and concern. You can be agents of mercy only because you yourselves have experienced the mercy, compassion and encouragement of God. Your visits are not so much about what you do as what God does through you.

Author James Kok, in his book *90% of Helping Is Just Showing Up*, argues that intimacy, not answers, is what people need most. As a deacon, you need to simply be present in people's lives and let God lead them (and you) into the next steps. Don't wait until you feel like some kind of "expert" before you visit people. Just show up, listen and share.

When you visit people in your congregation or community, you are bringing hope in Jesus' name. Remember there is no substitute for actually going out on some visits with an experienced deacon. After your visit, talk it over together.

Strategies for an effective visit

1. Wrap your visit in prayer. Pray before you visit; ask God to guide you. Share your uncertainties with God. Know what you are good at and focus there. Do not be afraid to say "I don't know" if you don't.
2. Listen! Listen! Listen! Come to listen and hear the person you are visiting. Don't come to "fix."
3. Ensure confidentiality. Assure the individual that the story is safe with you.
4. Point beyond yourself to God. You can do this by offering words of encouragement, a brief word from Scripture and prayer. Be sensitive to the nudging of the Spirit!
5. Problem-solve only when it is requested. State the difficulty together and together consider the most suitable options of response.

Who needs a visit?

1. A shut-in who has crippling arthritis.
2. Those who have long-term illnesses.
3. Someone without appropriate housing.

4. A church member who can't make ends meet.
5. An unemployed person in your neighborhood.
6. A person who feels lonely and left out in church.
7. An elderly person in the community whose children never visit.
8. A widow grieving the loss of her husband.
9. A couple who have just had their first baby.
10. A senior on his eightieth birthday.
11. A single parent having a tough time.
12. A child who has run away from home.
13. A person who has been abused.
14. A family on welfare trying to find work and make a new start.
15. An alcoholic looking for help.
16. A couple who overspends and needs to learn budgeting.

Learn how to listen

Listening is the gift you can give. It creates an atmosphere of trust and acceptance with the one you are listening to. Your gift of listening helps people put their thoughts and feelings into words, which is the first step toward helping themselves. Listening also helps people build relationships with each other and God. If we listen carefully, we can explore a variety of needs. And we will know what to pray when the time comes.

We use the following case study about Susan to learn some effective strategies for listening. As you read, imagine that Susan is a member of your church, and you are going to be her deacon. Imagine that you are about to meet with Susan. Think about some possible needs to listen for during your visit.

Susan is a thirty-six-year-old single parent of three children—David, thirteen; Sam, ten; Jane, eight. She divorced her husband three years ago after several years of neglect and abuse. Just after the divorce, Susan transferred her membership to our church. Last fall she went back to school to train as a bookkeeper. Although Susan started attending the women's Bible study group two years ago, she has been absent a lot lately. Because of the pressure of raising the children as a single parent, running the home and doing school work, she finds any other activity hard to fit in. She is often quite lonely. She has not made many friends, except for a few women in the Bible study.

Susan's ex-husband lives an hour away. He pays child support only occasionally. Susan receives supplementary assistance from the government. Her family lives forty-five minutes away and is not very involved with her. They are not happy with the divorce.

Two kinds of questions

One way to understand a person is by asking questions. Try asking open-ended questions that encourage longer answers instead of questions that can be answered with a yes or a no.

Closed: *Are you tired at the end of the day, Susan?*

Open: *How do you feel after a busy day?*

For reflection—What is the difference between these two ways of asking questions?

Reflect content and feelings

Here are some examples of reflecting content:

Susan: *No one comes to see me anymore.*

Deacon: *You haven't had a lot of visitors lately.*

Susan: *No I haven't. I wish I could see some of the women from my Bible study once in a while.*

Deacon: *You wish some of your friends would come.*

Here are some examples of reflecting feelings:

Susan: *No one comes to see me anymore.*

Deacon: *It sounds like you feel lonely.*

Susan: *Yes, I do. I see some people in my bookkeeping class but it isn't the same. I used to love going out. But, now I'm stuck at home.*

Deacon: *That seems to make you feel sad.*

For reflection—Why is it important to reflect feelings as well as content?

Listening for understanding

This conversation between Susan and her deacon takes place in a restaurant over lunch. The first few minutes are spent talking about the restaurant, the weather and what to order.

Susan: *I don't go out for lunch much.*

Deacon: *I guess that it's hard to do in your busy life.*

Susan: *I can't really afford it. Sometimes I go out with the kids on their birthday. That way they have something special.*

Deacon: *Do you get a chance to go out with your parents and your family?*

Susan: *Not really. We don't talk much since the divorce. They were pretty against it, you know. I go to family get-togethers. But I always feel like I'm the black sheep . . . and I guess I am.*

Deacon: *It sounds like you feel abandoned.*

Susan: *Sometimes. But I can't let it bother me. I'm too busy. By the time I get home from school, make supper, run*

> *a load of laundry, clean up, help the kids with papers, do my own homework, drive them to sports . . . it's hard to find the energy. It's hardest late at night.*

Deacon: *What kind of thoughts come to you then?*

Susan: *The kids. I worry about them. We've just moved for the second time in five years. I needed to do it in order to get away from Tom and be close enough to school, but I'm concerned about the effect all of this is having on my children.*

Deacon: *All the moving is hard on them.*

Susan: *Yes, it is. They had to change schools in the middle of the year, and they had a hard time making new friends. Stephen is in junior high and friends are very important to him. He's really angry with me about moving.*

Deacon: *How does that leave you feeling?*

Susan: *Oh, I just wish I could make everyone happy. But my kids are hurting and there's not much I can do about it. I can't stop thinking about it. Every time I see Stephen feeling upset, I feel worse.*

Deacon: *This situation seems to be really eating at you.*

For reflection—How could you tell the deacon was really paying attention in the conversation? In their conversation, find an example of an open-ended question, reflecting content, reflecting feelings.

Listen to explore needs

A few days after their lunch conversation, the deacon invites Susan and the kids over for a picnic with several other families. Since Susan had mentioned her financial struggles during the previous conversation, the deacon asks her to jot down her income and expenses so they can discuss her finances in more detail during their next visit. The following is part of the conversation during a visit three weeks later.

Deacon: *Last time you mentioned that your ex-husband is supposed to send child support of $100 per month, but he doesn't always do it. Doesn't that mean your finances are pretty tight sometimes?*

Susan: *It's worse on special days and when school starts. There is just nothing left.*

Deacon: *I would think that finances create a lot of pressure for you. One thing we do as deacons is pitch in to help. Maybe you could use some help with—*

Susan: *(interrupts) I don't know. I don't want everyone to know I'm getting help.*

Deacon: *I can appreciate that. That's why we don't tell anyone. This information is strictly confidential . . . only the deacons know.*

Susan: *(hesitantly) Oh . . .*

Deacon: *Does that help?*

Susan: *Yes. But I'm still not sure I need the help.*

Deacon: *Why don't we begin by looking at some of those numbers?*

Susan: *Oh yeah. I have it right here*

Deacon: *As I look at these figures, they show that you just break even. That's a tight squeeze. How do you manage when the car breaks down or when your ex-husband doesn't come through?*

Susan: *I don't (laughs). Listen to me, here I am laughing about it. Usually I get upset and start crying. Sometimes I babysit or get a part-time job. I juggle a lot.*

Deacon: *Do you feel that you need a regular amount each month to help you just break even?*

For reflection—How did the deacon help Susan feel more comfortable about sharing her financial needs?

How to build prayer into a visit

Our visits need to be wrapped in prayer—not to make the visit "Christian" but because we need to bring the person's needs and our own needs before God. Building prayer into visits occurs naturally when we focus on listening and understanding. Notice in the following example that Susan's deacon doesn't simply pray for her; instead the deacon helps bring her specific needs before God. The prayer grows out of the understanding that develops throughout the visit. The following conversation takes place after Susan and her deacon have discussed her finances and her struggles as a single parent.

Deacon: *I really appreciate your willingness to share with me. I've learned a lot and yet I feel like I still have a lot to learn. You need a lot of wisdom and strength in your situation. I want you to know I pray for you*

Susan: *I sure could use it sometimes.*

Deacon: *Would you appreciate a time of prayer right now? We've talked about lots of feelings and some struggles. Would you like to share these with God in prayer?*

Susan: *Sure, I guess so.*

Deacon: *In my prayer I would like to ask God to keep you close and provide you with wisdom. Is there anything else you'd like us to pray about?*

Susan: *How to deal with my son's anger. And I just want some friends to visit with.*

Deacon: *We'll invite God to help you with your son's anger. Let's ask God to lead you to a friend or two. And I'd like to pray that the children would feel at home soon.*

Susan: *That would be good.*

Deacon: *Okay, let's pray . . .*

For reflection—How did the deacon effectively build prayer into the visit with Susan?

When to pray

1. Prayer should be a natural part of the visit. Because prayer cannot be programmed beforehand, you'll need to determine the proper moment to pray during each visit. That judgment depends on the person's needs, not yours. In other words, pray when you sense that the person you're visiting is ready, not when you are ready. Careful listening will help you ascertain when prayer is appropriate. Let prayer be a natural part of your conversation, not an intrusion or interruption.

2. Don't artificially tack prayer onto a visit. Prayer is not a vehicle for introducing your Christian viewpoint. The entire visit is an opportunity to demonstrate your love and concern. If that doesn't shine through the rest of the conversation, prayer will not "make it Christian."

3. Although it is a common practice to close a visit with prayer, consider occasionally praying with people at other times during the visit. Prayer is not a technique for closing a visit. If you always close with prayer, the people you're visiting might come to look on the prayer as a way to say goodbye rather than a way to communicate with God. They may even feel disappointment when you mention prayer, because it signals that you

will be leaving. Remember that prayer can come appropriately at any time during a visit.

4. Avoid the temptation of using prayer as a means to manipulate. For example, praying, "Heavenly Father, I come before you today asking that you would bring about a change of heart in Susan, so that she will become willing to _____." This is merely an attempt to force Susan's hand by arousing feelings of guilt. A prayer of this sort will have negative results. If, on the other hand, Susan expresses a desire to pray for a change of heart, such a prayer could be appropriate. In that case the prayer is coming from Susan's expressed needs, not your own agenda.

Introducing the prayer

Initiating prayer is awkward for some people. What do you say when you sense that prayer is appropriate? If you want to avoid the simple declaration, "let's pray," try one of the following.

- "Would you appreciate prayer right now?"
- "We have talked about this problem and you expressed a lot of feelings. Would you like to share these with God in prayer?"
- "You set a personal goal for yourself. Would you like to ask God for help?"
- "I'm really glad things have gone well with you this week. Shall we share our thanks with God in prayer?"

These introductions leave the individual with the choice. Prayer needs to be a willing response.

When someone says "No"

Much of the time, when you ask people if they would like to pray, your suggestion will be welcome. Of course, they may also say no. On those occasions, many people will offer a reason. Whatever the reason, you need not become defensive or think that you are being rejected. Remember that as your relationship develops there might be other occasions when the person will feel more open to prayer. Be patient!

What to pray about

Pray about the need that suggested prayer in the first place. This will enable you to focus the prayer, which will also make it more meaningful for the other person. Both of you will benefit if you are clear about the needs you bring to God before you pray. The following example shows how to ensure that both of you understand which needs will be included in prayer.

Mrs. Thompson is facing surgery the next morning. She tells you that she is worried and afraid. By asking open-ended questions, you encourage Mrs. Thompson to express her real concerns. After listening to her, you ask if she would like to pray, and she says yes. Your conversation might go something like this.

Deacon: *Before we pray, what are some of your thoughts and feelings right now?*

Mrs. T: *I am worried that after surgery is over, I won't be able to take care of my children. I feel so alone right now.*

Deacon: *You'd like us to pray about your fears of loneliness and your worries that something might happen tomorrow that would prevent you from being a good mother to your children?*

Mrs. T: *Yes. I know I shouldn't feel this way and think these thoughts, but what if I die?*

Deacon: *It sounds as if we should ask God to help you as you struggle with this fear of death. Is there anything else you would like to share with God in prayer?*

Mrs. T.: *No, these are my chief concerns.*

By inviting Mrs. Thompson to share her concerns, you have information to use in building a prayer that meets her needs.

When someone asks you to pray

Occasionally someone will request the prayer. When that happens, you might be tempted to immediately fold your hands and begin praying. But remember that prayer should meet the person's needs. A good response includes finding out more about the person in need. You might say something like this: "I would be glad to pray with you. But before I do, I'd like you to share with me you what you're thinking and what your needs are at this time. That way we can share them better with God." The point is not to stall but to provide better quality ministry.

Sharing words of hope

Deacons are invited to encourage people with words that bring hope, and with deeds that bring joy into their lives. Can you think of words that bring hope to people? Sometimes it's hard to know what to say. Sometimes it best to say nothing and simply be with the person.

Words that refresh

"May the Lord show mercy to the household of Onesiphorus, because he often refreshed me and was not ashamed of my chains" (2 Tim. 1:16 NIV 1984). Paul honors Onesiphorus as one who stood by him in prison. The word refresh in the Bible has several meanings—physical refreshment, encouragement and spiritual renewal—and comes from deeds and words.

Deacons are encouragers too. During your visit you will find yourself needing to share a word of encouragement in a variety of situations.

- A young couple—trying to make ends meet—need a word of encouragement to stick with the budget plan.
- A single parent needs a word of encouragement as she tries to cope with the demands of raising two children.
- A widow needs to be encouraged to grieve the loss of her husband and lay that grief before the Lord.
- An unemployed person needs words of encouragement as he looks for new work but is constantly faced with closed doors.

Speak God's Word

As a deacon, you have an inexhaustible resource for bringing words of hope. But only when you draw from the riches of the Bible yourself will you be able to speak God's word of comfort to others. For that reason it's important to spend time in prayer and meditation of God's Word before you go and visit. Choose a Psalm to reflect on—perhaps Psalm 23 or Psalm 62. These speak of God's leading and of how God can help us find peace in the midst of turmoil. Immerse yourself in the words before you go out and visit. While you are there, listen with all of your heart. Listen for content and feelings. Pay attention to expressions of being overwhelmed by grief. Invite the person to pour out her heart to God like the psalmist in Psalm 62.

Which passage?

The more you immerse yourselves in God's Word, the more you will be able to share appropriate words of hope and encouragement in the varying circumstances of diaconal ministry.

- Psalm 23; Hebrews 13: 5–6 – God will not forsake us in our time of pain.
- Psalm 61 – Asking God to lift us out of our difficulty.
- Psalm 62 – Finding peace in the midst of turmoil.
- Psalm 63 – The need for prayer.
- Psalm 90 – Our hope is in God.
- Psalm 103 – God's great love for us.
- Philippians 4:6–7; 1 Peter 5:7 – Bring your anxieties to God; He cares for you.
- Romans 5:10–11; 1 John 1:9 – Forgiveness is a gift and a promise.
- Galatians 4:5; Romans 8:15 – God is our Father (Abba).
- 2 Corinthians 8:1–7; 9:6–7 – The joy of giving generously to God.
- Galatians 6:9; Isaiah 41:10 – Don't give up; God will strengthen you.
- Romans 8:1; Isaiah 1:18 – There is no guilt too great for God.
- Romans 4:20–21; 1 John 5:14–15 – Trust in God; claim God's promises.

What is your favorite passage?

This is a good question to ask when you are on a visit. People often have in mind Bible passages that especially speak to them when they are struggling. Asking this question allows them to repeat God's own words of comfort. Also ask, "Why is this passage especially helpful to you?"

Be ready to share your own favorite as you visit and why it is special or meaningful to you.

What can you do to help?

Here are suggestions for caring for those who are suffering from long-term (possibly terminal) illnesses.

I am a married young woman struggling to beat cancer. My husband and I have three children: a baby, a preschooler and a first grader. Since I am severely ill, we depend on our friends for survival. Over the months, so many of my friends have asked, "what can I do?" Here are some ideas.

1. *Cook a meal for my family, but offer a choice of two courses (because one week, we had tuna noodle casserole four nights in a row) and bring it in disposable containers (because if I can't return your dishes, I cry in my powerlessness).*

2. *Make your offer specific. Say, "I want to come over Monday at three o'clock to bake cookies and clean your pantry shelf." If you say, "Call me any time for anything," I don't know what you want to do or when you are free. And I probably won't ask.*

3. *Offer to babysit—even if my husband and I stay home. This gives us the freedom of a private adult life in the place my illness can cope with.*

4. *Help with holidays, birthdays and anniversaries. Ask if there are any special gifts or cards or wrapping papers you could pick up for me. How many times I have wanted to give my husband a special thank you card or put up a holiday decoration, but have been unable!*

5. *Take snapshots of my children over the months. This gives me a feeling that there are permanent records of the temporary happenings I must miss.*

6. *Allow me to feel sad or prepared for the worst. One of the most difficult problems of having a serious illness is that everyone wants to encourage me; but sometimes the luxury of having a good cry with a friend who will allow it lets the tension escape—once the dam has broken.*

7. *Even if the joke is terrible, tell it! Share your humor. Bring the magazine and read aloud. Describe what is funny out there. It may not tickle my ribs today, but tomorrow I may relish it. Speak to the part of me that is more alive than dead, for that is the real me.*

8. *Touch me. The isolation of being an invalid makes the power of love even sweeter.*

9. *Say the word cancer around me, and talk about the real life you are living. This helps me feel less like an untouchable and like I'm still involved with the world. One of the hardest things about being an invalid is the problem of being isolated from what's going on. If you don't talk to me about life outside, I am left to discuss with my husband only illness and television, and this is hard.*

10. *Encourage your husband to come over to visit my husband in the evenings. One of the greatest gifts I have is my husband, and yet my illness has eliminated many of his pleasures. How happy I am when I hear him laughing with a friend or cheering Monday night football with a pal.*

11. *Pray for me and say so. The fact that you have faith gives me faith.*

Helping new deacons make a smooth entrance

Newly elected deacons can best be supported by a mentor—experienced deacons who will help them answer the practical questions that will come up in their work. A mentor is able to not only share his or her experiences, but also accompany the new deacon on visits. New deacons who are connected to an experienced deacon are ready to do ministry much sooner than those who are left to discover the task on their own. The diaconate could also do the following to assist the transition:

1. Provide a written task description.
2. Provide new deacon training.
3. Explain how to respond to needs in the church and community.
4. Detail the activities in which the diaconate participates throughout the year.
5. Encourage opportunities to develop the particular gifts that a deacon brings.
6. Nurture each person's spiritual growth with regular prayer and devotion.

Discussion

1. Would you ask for help? Let's face it. Most people don't call the diaconate for help. Why is that?

   - If you had a financial need or some other need— loneliness, sadness, sickness—would you call in the deacons for help? Why or why not?

   - What would make you hesitate?

2. Learn how to listen. Discuss the following questions as you reflect on the conversation between the deacon and Susan in the section "Listen for understanding."

   - Why are open-ended questions helpful in this conversation?
   - How can you effectively build prayer into a visit?

- If you were Susan, how would you feel about the visit?

3. The parts of the body can be a helpful reminder of what deacons are to do.

   - Describe how each body part can help you carry out your diaconal ministry (ears, eyes, mouth, heart, hands, arms, feet, knees).

4. When you visit the sick, review the section "What can I do to help?" Imagine that you are a deacon who visits with a woman who has cancer.

   - What is the first thing that you should try to do?

   - What are some of the needs of this family?

   - What could the deacons and the congregation do to meet the family's needs?

Visiting is the heart of the deacon's work. In connecting with people one-on-one we share the mercy of Christ. With a partner, take some time in the next couple of months to visit people in your congregation and your community. Get a feeling for what is involved. After each visit, reflect with your partner about what happened,

- How did the visit go? If not well, why not?
- How did you arrange the visit?
- How did you prepare yourself?
- Did you offer words of encouragement? Did you build prayer into the visit? How and when?
- What would you do differently?[67]

Appendix E:

Scripture Passages for Deacons

This list is not exhaustive. The passages are not listed in any order or priority. For deacons who are searching, the list may be a good place to start.

Exodus 22:21–22 "You shall not wrong a sojourner or oppress him, for you were sojourners in the land of Egypt. You shall not mistreat any widow or fatherless child."

Leviticus 19:9–10 "When you reap the harvest of your land, you shall not reap your field right up to its edge, neither shall you gather the gleanings after your harvest. And you shall not strip your vineyard bare, neither shall you gather the fallen grapes of your vineyard. You shall leave them for the poor and for the sojourner: I am the LORD your God."

Deuteronomy 16:9–12 "You shall count seven weeks. Begin to count the seven weeks from the time the sickle is first put to the standing grain. Then you shall keep the Feast of Weeks to the LORD your God with the tribute of a freewill offering from your hand, which you shall give as the LORD your God blesses you. And you shall rejoice before the LORD your God, you and your son and your daughter, your male servant and your female servant, the Levite who is within your towns, the sojourner, the fatherless, and the widow who are among you, at the place that the LORD your God will choose, to make his name dwell there. You shall remember that you were a slave in Egypt; and you shall be careful to observe these statutes."

Deuteronomy 24:17–22 "You shall not pervert the justice due to the sojourner or to the fatherless, or take a widow's garment in pledge, but you shall remember that you were a slave in Egypt and the LORD your God redeemed you from there; therefore I command you to do this.

"When you reap your harvest in your field and forget a sheaf in the field, you shall not go back to get it. It shall be for the sojourner, the fatherless, and the widow, that the LORD your God may bless you in all the work of your hands. When you beat your olive trees, you shall not go over them again. It shall be for the sojourner, the fatherless, and the widow. When you gather the grapes of your vineyard, you shall not strip it afterward. It shall be for the sojourner, the fatherless, and the widow. You shall remember that you were a slave in the land of Egypt; therefore I command you to do this."

Psalm 41:1 "Blessed is the one who considers the poor! In the day of trouble the LORD delivers him."

Psalm 112:4–5 "Light dawns in the darkness for the upright; he is gracious, merciful, and righteous. It is well with the man who deals generously and lends; who conducts his affairs with justice."

Psalm 112:9 "He has distributed freely; he has given to the poor; his righteousness endures forever; his horn is exalted in honor."

Psalm 146:5, 7–9 "Blessed is he . . . who executes justice for the oppressed, who gives food to the hungry. The LORD sets the prisoners free; the LORD opens the eyes of the blind. The LORD lifts up those who are bowed down; the LORD loves the righteous. The LORD watches over the sojourners; he upholds the widow and the fatherless, but the way of the wicked he brings to ruin."

Proverbs 14:20–21 "The poor is disliked even by his neighbor, but the rich has many friends. Whoever despises his neighbor is a sinner, but blessed is he who is generous to the poor."

Proverbs 28:27 "Whoever gives to the poor will not want, but he who hides his eyes will get many a curse."

Isaiah 3:13–15 "The LORD has taken his place to contend; he stands to judge peoples. The LORD will enter into judgment with the elders and princes of his people: 'It is you who have devoured the vineyard, the spoil of the poor is in your houses. What do you mean by crushing my people, by grinding the face of the poor?' declares the Lord GOD of hosts."

Isaiah 58:5–7 "Is such the fast that I choose, a day for a person to humble himself? Is it to bow down his head like a reed, and to spread sackcloth and ashes under him? Will you call this a fast, and a day acceptable to the LORD? Is not this the fast that I choose: to loose the bonds of wickedness, to undo the straps of the yoke, to let the oppressed go free, and to break every yoke? Is it not to share your bread with the hungry and bring the homeless poor into your house; when you see the naked, to cover him, and not to hide yourself from your own flesh?"

Jeremiah 7:5–6 "For if you truly amend your ways and your deeds, if you truly execute justice one with another, if you do not oppress the sojourner, the fatherless, or the widow, or shed innocent blood in this place, and if you do not go after other gods to your own harm . . ."

Ezekiel 22:7 "Father and mother are treated with contempt in you; the sojourner suffers extortion in your midst; the fatherless and the widow are wronged in you."

Ezekiel 22:29 "The people of the land have practiced extortion and committed robbery. They have oppressed the poor and needy, and have extorted from the sojourner without justice."

Amos 2:6–7 "Thus says the LORD: 'For three transgressions of Israel, and for four, I will not revoke the punishment, because they sell the righteous for silver, and the needy for a pair of sandals—those who trample the head of the poor into the dust of the earth and turn aside the way of the afflicted; a man and his father go in to the same girl, so that my holy name is profaned.'"

Amos 8:4–7 "Hear this, you who trample on the needy and bring the poor of the land to an end, saying, 'When will the new moon be over, that we may sell grain? And the Sabbath, that we may offer wheat for sale, that we may make the ephah small and the shekel great and deal deceitfully with false balances, that we may buy the poor for silver and the needy for a pair of sandals and sell the chaff of the wheat?' The LORD has sworn by the pride of Jacob: 'Surely I will never forget any of their deeds.'"

Micah 2:2 "They covet fields and seize them, and houses, and take them away; they oppress a man and his house, a man and his inheritance."

Zechariah 7:9–10 "Thus says the LORD of hosts, Render true judgments, show kindness and mercy to one another, do not oppress the widow, the fatherless, the sojourner, or the poor, and let none of you devise evil against another in your heart."

Matthew 10:37–42 "Whoever loves father or mother more than me is not worthy of me, and whoever loves son or daughter more than me is not worthy of me. And whoever does not take his cross and follow me is not worthy of me. Whoever finds his life will lose it, and whoever loses his life for my sake will find it. Whoever receives you receives me, and whoever receives me receives him who sent me. The one who receives a prophet because he is a prophet will receive a prophet's reward, and the one who receives a righteous person because he is a righteous person will receive a righteous person's reward. And whoever gives one of these little ones even a cup of cold water because he is a disciple, truly, I say to you, he will by no means lose his reward."

Matthew 18:32–34 "Then his master summoned him and said to him, 'You wicked servant! I forgave you all that debt because you pleaded with me. And should not you have had mercy on your fellow servant, as I had mercy on you?' And in anger his master delivered him to the jailers, until he should pay all his debt."

Matthew 25:31–40 "When the Son of Man comes in his glory, and all the angels with him, then he will sit on his glorious throne. Before him will be gathered all the nations, and he will separate people one from another as a shepherd separates the sheep from the goats. And he will place the sheep on his right, but the goats on the left. Then the King will say to those on his right, 'Come, you who are blessed by my Father, inherit the kingdom prepared for you from the foundation of the world. For I was hungry and you gave me food, I was thirsty and you gave me drink, I was a stranger and you welcomed me, I was naked and you clothed me, I was sick and you visited me, I was in prison and you came to me.' Then the righteous will answer him, saying, 'Lord, when did we see you hungry and feed you, or thirsty and give you drink? And when did we see you a stranger and welcome you, or naked and clothe you? And when did we see you sick or in prison and visit you?' And the King will answer them, 'Truly, I say to you, as you did it to one of the least of these my brothers, you did it to me.'"

Luke 1:51–53 "He has shown strength with his arm; he has scattered the proud in the thoughts of their hearts; he has brought down the mighty from their thrones and exalted those of humble estate; he has filled the hungry with good things, and the rich he has sent away empty."

Luke 4:18 "The Spirit of the Lord is upon me, because he has anointed me to proclaim good news to the poor. He has sent me to proclaim liberty to the captives and recovering of sight to the blind, to set at liberty those who are oppressed."

Luke 6:32–36 "If you love those who love you, what benefit is that to you? For even sinners love those who love them. And if you do good to those who do good to you, what benefit is that to you? For even sinners do the same. And if you lend to those from whom you expect to receive, what credit is that to you? Even sinners lend to sinners, to get back the same amount. But love your enemies, and do good, and lend, expecting nothing in return, and your reward will be great, and you will be sons of the Most High, for he is kind to the ungrateful and the evil. Be merciful, even as your Father is merciful."

Acts 4:32–34 "Now the full number of those who believed were of one heart and soul, and no one said that any of the things that belonged to him was his own, but they had everything in common. And with great power the apostles were giving their testimony to the resurrection of the Lord Jesus, and great grace was upon them all. There was not a needy person among them, for as many as were owners of lands or houses sold them and brought the proceeds of what was sold."

Acts 6:1–5 "In those days when the number of disciples was increasing, the Grecian Jews among them complained against those of the Aramaic-speaking community because their widows were being overlooked in the daily distribution of food. So the Twelve gathered all the disciples together and said, 'It would not be right for us to neglect the ministry of the word of God in order to wait on tables. Brothers, choose seven men from among you who are known to be full of the Spirit and wisdom. We will turn this responsibility over to them and will give our attention to prayer and the ministry of the word.'"(NIV 1984)

Romans 12:6, 8 "If a man's gift . . . is encouraging, let him encourage; if it is contributing to the needs of others, let him give generously; if it is leadership, let him govern diligently; if it is showing mercy, let him do it cheerfully." (NIV 1984)

1 Corinthians 12:28 "And God has appointed in the church first apostles, second prophets, third teachers, then miracles, then gifts of healing, helping, administrating."

Galatians 2:10 "Only, they asked us to remember the poor, the very thing I was eager to do."

Colossians 3:12 "Put on then, as God's chosen ones, holy and beloved, compassionate hearts, kindness, humility, meekness, and patience."

1 Timothy 6:17–19 "As for the rich in this present age, charge them not to be haughty, nor to set their hopes on the uncertainty of riches, but on God, who richly provides us with everything to enjoy. They are to do good, to be rich in good works, to be generous and ready to share, thus storing up treasure for themselves as a good foundation for the future, so that they may take hold of that which is truly life."

Hebrews 13:2 "Do not neglect to show hospitality to strangers, for thereby some have entertained angels unawares."

James 1:27 "Religion that is pure and undefiled before God, the Father, is this: to visit orphans and widows in their affliction, and to keep oneself unstained from the world."

James 2:14–17 "What good is it, my brothers, if someone says he has faith but does not have works? Can that faith save him? If a brother or sister is poorly clothed and lacking in daily food, and one of you says to them, 'Go in peace, be warmed and filled,' without giving them the things needed for the body, what good is that? So also faith by itself, if it does not have works, is dead."

James 4:17 "So whoever knows the right thing to do and fails to do it, for him it is sin."

1 John 3:17–18 "But if anyone has the world's goods and sees his brother in need, yet closes his heart against him, how does God's love abide in him? Little children, let us not love in word or talk but in deed and in truth."

Scripture on Caring with Compassion

Afflictions	Are often providential—Ps. 119:67, 71, 75
	God will deliver—Ps. 34:19
Anxiety	Is relieved through prayer—Phil. 4:6–7
	Remember, God cares for you—1 Pet. 5:7
Assurance	Eternal life promised—John 3:16–17
	You can be sure—1 John 5:11–13
Comfort	Jesus, the Good Shepherd—Ps. 23
	He will never forsake you—Heb. 13:5–6
Discouragement	Don't give up—Gal. 6:9
	God will help and strengthen—Isa. 41:10
Emptiness	Christ can satisfy—Ps. 107:8–9
	He will fulfill your desires—Ps. 37:4–5
Forgiveness	Promised—Ps. 32:5; 1 John 1:9
Guilt	No condemnation—Rom. 8:1
	No sin is too great—Isa. 1:18
Judgment	All are accountable—Rom. 14:12; Heb. 9:27
Loneliness	His presence promised—Heb. 13:5–6
	There is joy in His presence—Ps. 16:11

Suffering	Suffering has profit—Heb. 12:6–11
	God's grace is sufficient—2 Cor. 12:9–10
	It is to be expected—1 Pet. 2:19–23
	It deepens the faith—1 Pet. 1:6–7
Temptations	How to avoid them—Matt. 26:41
	What causes failure—James 1:13–14
Victory	Is in Christ—Phil. 4:13
	Your inner resource—1 John 4:4
	Seek God's help—1 Cor. 10:13
Worry	God will provide—Phil. 4:19
	Have faith in Him—Rom. 4:20–21
	Claim His promises—1 John 5:4, 15

Appendix F: Bibliography

Aldrich, Joseph C. *Gentle Persuasion*. Portland: Multnomah Press, 1988.

Barclay, William. *Daily Study Bible Series*. NavPress Wordsearch CD-ROM.

Bainton, Roland H. *The Reformation of the Sixteenth Century*. Boston: Beacon Press, 1952.

Biéler, André. *The Social Humanism of Calvin*. Richmond: John Knox Press, 1964.

Berkhoef, Gerard and Lester DeKoster. *The Deacons Handbook*. Grand Rapids: Christian Library's Press, 1980.

Blumin, Stuart. *The Emergence of the Middle Class*. New York: Cambridge University Press, 1989.

Boice, James M. *Commentary on Romans*. Grand Rapids, MI: Baker Book House, 1998.

Bonhoeffer, Dietrich. *The Cost of Discipleship*. New York: Macmillan, 1963.

Bouwsma, William J. *John Calvin, A Sixteenth Century Portrait*. New York: Oxford University Press, 1988.

Brussat, Frederic and Mary Ann, eds. *Spiritual Literacy.* New York: Scribner, 1996.

Fauble, Douglas. *A Leader Among Servants.* Chicago: Chicagoland Diaconal Task Force, 1989.

Gottlieb, Dan. "Encounters with Someone Who is Different." *Philadelphia Inquirer,* April 28, 2008.

Henry, Matthew. *Commentary on the Whole Bible.* Iowa Falls, IA: World Bible Publishers.

Innes, William C. *Social Concern in Calvin's Geneva.* Allison Park, PA: Pickwick Publications, 1983.

Keller, Timothy. *Diaconal Ministry: A Video Training Course.* Philadelphia: Westminster Media, 1987.

Klay, Robin, et al. *Inflation, Poortalk, and the Gospel.* Valley Forge: Judson Press, 1981.

Koyama, Kosuke. *Waterbuffalo Theology.* Maryknoll, NY: Orbis Books, 1974.

Langberg, Diane. "The Fellowship of His Suffering," PCA Mercy Ministry Conference, April 21, 2007, Atlanta, GA.

Leverett, Mo. "Compelled by the Gospel to Lay Down Our Lives," *byFaith,* October 7, 2005.

MacDonald, Gordon. *Ordering Your Private World*. Nashville: Thomas Nelson Publishers, 1985.

McKee, Elsie Anne. *Diakonia in the Classical Reformed Tradition and Today*. Grand Rapids: Eerdmans Publishing, 1989.

Monter, William E. *Calvin's Geneva*. London: John Wiley and Sons Inc., 1975.

New English Hymnal. Louisville, KY: Westminster John Knox Press, 1971.

Nouwen, Henri J.M. *Reaching Out*. Garden City, NY: Image Books, 1966.

Olson, Jeannine. *Calvin and Social Welfare*. New York: Associated University Press, 1986.

Ogden, Greg. *The New Reformation*. Grand Rapids: Zondervan Publishing, 1992.

Perkins, Spencer and Chris Rice. *More Than Equals*. Downers Grove, IL: InterVarsity Press, 1993.

Petty, Krista. "Tenth Presbyterian Church: A Model of Long-Term Engagement in the City And multiplying the efforts through collaborative training." (fastennetwork.org, 2007).

Pierson, Jim, *No Disabled Souls*. Cincinnati, Ohio, The Standard Publishing Co., 1998.

Potter, G.R. and M. Greengrass. *John Calvin*. New York: St. Martin's Press, 1983.

Psalter Hymnal. Grand Rapids: Christian Reformed Publishing House, 1959.

Ryken, Philip. *Commentary on Luke*. P&R Publishing, Phillipsburg, NJ, 2009.

Schlabach, Gerald. *And Who Is My Neighbor?* Scottdale, PA: Herald Press, 1990.

Stob, George. *Deacons and Evangelism*. Grand Rapids: Christian Reformed Publishing House, 1978.

Vandezande, Ben. *Servant Leaders: A Practical Guide for Deacons*. Grand Rapids, MI, CRC Publications, 2000.

Van Klinken, Jaap. *Diakonia*. Grand Rapids: Eerdmans Publishing, 1989.

Wilson, Marlene. *How to Mobilize Church Volunteers*. Minneapolis: Augsburg Publishing, 1986.

NOTES

1. Joseph C. Aldrich, *Gentle Persuasion* (Portland: Multnomah Press, 1988), 109.

2. Alan Jay Lerner and Frederick Loewe, *My Fair Lady*, Columbia Records, 1956.

3. Gerard Berghoef and Lester DeKoster, *The Deacons Handbook* (Grand Rapids, MI: CLP, 1983), 215.

4. Kosuke Koyama, *Waterbuffalo Theology* (Maryknoll, NY: Orbis Books, 1974), 107.

5. Philip G. Ryken, *Reformed Expository Commentary, Luke, Volume I* (P&R Publishing, Phillipsburg, NJ), 390.

6. William Barclay, *Daily Study Bible Series*, NavPress Wordsearch CD-ROM.

7. Gerald Schlabach, *And Who Is My Neighbor?* (Scottdale, PA: Herald Press, 1990), 77.

8. Barclay, op. cit.

9. Matthew Henry, *Commentary on the Whole Bible* (Iowa Falls, IA: World Bible Publishers, 1983), Vol. V, 686.

10. Barclay, op. cit.

11. Spencer Perkins and Chris Rice, *More Than Equals* (Downers Grove, IL: InterVarsity Press, 1993), 62.

12. Ibid, 63.

13. Timothy Keller, *Diaconal Ministry: A Video Training Course* (Philadelphia, Westminster Media, 1987).

14. Henri J. M. Nouwen, *Reaching Out* (Colorado Springs, CO: Image Publishing), 65.

15. James M. Boice, *Romans, Volume 4: The New Humanity.* (Grand Rapids, MI: Baker Book House, 1997).

16. The Greeting at Tenth Presbyterian Church.

17. Institute for Public Policy Study, *Homelessness in Philadelphia.* (Philadelphia: Temple University, 1989), 38.

18. Ibid, iii.

19. Ibid.

20. Stuart Blumin, *The Emergence of the Middle Class* (New York: Cambridge University Press, 1989), 221.

21. *The Doctrines of Grace, The Five Solas,* and *The Westminster Confession of Faith.*

22. From an interview. Adapted with permission from the original publisher, from the essay "Tenth Presbyterian Church: A model of long-term engagement in the city and multiplying the efforts through collaborative training," by Krista Petty (FASTENnetwork.org, 2007).

23. Compiled by David Apple from hundreds of interviews with homeless persons.

24. Mission Statement, September 18, 1988, in *Tenth Presbyterian Church Organization Manual,* 1.

25. The focus group consisted of Phil Beauford, Gerald Carter, Vivian Dow, Gerald Gardner, Cathy Giaimo, Joe Giaimo, Betsy Kline, Kevin Little, Tina Simon, Alan Petrongolo, Mike Waltz and Glenn Wesley.

26. "The Fellowship of His Suffering," PCA Mercy Ministry Conference, April 21, 2007, Atlanta, GA.

27. Ibid.

28. *New English Hymnal* (Louisville, KY: Westminster John Knox Press, 1971), 200.

29. Mo Leverett, "Compelled by the Gospel to Lay Down Our Lives," *byFaith*, October 7, 2005.

30. From ACTS Ministries' archives, source unknown.

31. Gordon MacDonald, *Ordering Your Private World* (Nashville, TN: Nelson Publishers, 1985), 78.

32. Quoted by the Rev. Tom Skinner at the 1978 Association for Public Justice Conference, Dordt College, Sioux Center, Iowa.

33. William C. Innes, *Social Concern in Calvin's Geneva* (Allison Park, PA: Pickwick Publications, 1983), 23.

34. Ibid, 14.

35. G.W.H. Lampe, "Diakonia in the Early Church," in James I. McCord and T. H. L. Parker, Editors. *Service in Christ: Essays Presented to Karl Barth on His 80th Birthday* (Grand Rapids: Eerdmans Publishing, 1986), 50.

36. Basil Hall, "Diakonia in Martin Bucer," in McCord, op. cit., 90.

37. Douglas Fauble, *A Leader Among Servants* (Chicago: Chicagoland Diaconal Task Force, 1989), 59.

38. André Biéler, *The Social Humanism of Calvin* (Richmond: John Knox Press, 1964), 36.

39. Elsie Anne McKee, *Diakonia in the Classical Reformed Tradition and Today* (Grand Rapids: Eerdmans Publishing, 1989), 39.

40. Jeannine Olson, *Calvin and Social Welfare* (New York: Associated University Press, 1986), 184.

41. Innes, op. cit., 149.

42. John Calvin, *Institutes of the Christian Religion*, Translation by Ford Lewis Battles (Philadelphia: Westminster Press, 1960), 960.

43. Roland H. Bainton, *The Reformation of the Sixteenth Century* (Boston: Beacon Press, 1952), 117.

44. G.R. Potter and M. Greengrass, *John Calvin* (New York: St. Martin's Press, 1983), 74.

45. Bouman, op. cit., 116.

46. Biéler, op. cit., 65.

47. Fauble, op. cit, 31.

48. Lewis Smedes, *The Reformed Journal*, January 1969 in George Stob, Editor, *Deacons and Evangelism* (Grand Rapids: Christian Reformed Publishing House, 1978), 89.

49. George Stob, Editor, *Deacons and Evangelism*, (Grand Rapids: Christian Reformed Publishing House, 1978), 89.

50. Stob, op. cit., 88.

51. *The Book of Church Order of the Presbyterian Church in America,* (Christian Education and Publications, Lawrenceville, GA, 2012), 9.1.

52. "Biblical Guidelines for Mercy Ministry in the PCA," published 1987, http://www.pcahistory.org/pca/2-414.html.

53. *The Book of Church Order of the Presbyterian Church in America,* op. cit., 9.7.

54. *Webster's New Collegiate Dictionary,* (Springfield, MA: G. & C. Merriam Company, 1975).

55. *The Book of Church Order of The Presbyterian Church in America*, op. cit., 9.2.

56. *Heidelberg Catechism,* Lord's Day XLII, Question and Answer 1 (*Psalter Hymnal,* Grand Rapids: Christian Reformed Publishing House, 1959), 22.

57. Dietrich Bonhoeffer, *Life Together*, (New York: Harper and Row, 1952), 97.

58. Henri Nouwen, *The Wounded Healer*, (Garden City, NY: Image Books, 1979), 88.

59. *Heidelberg Catechism,* Lord's Day XLII, Question and Answer 111 (*Psalter Hymnal,* Grand Rapids: Christian Reformed Publishing House, 1959), 40.

60. Adapted from Jim Pierson, *No Disabled Souls.* (Cincinnati, Ohio, The Standard Publishing Co., 1998), 62-64.

61. Dan Gottlieb, "Encounters with Someone Who Is Different," *Philadelphia Inquirer,* April 28, 2008.

62. I thank my friend Gary Burlingame, especially, and others from MercyNet, who helped me with some of the "how to minister" segments.

63. Timothy Keller, *Diaconal Ministry: A Video Training Course* (Philadelphia, Westminster Media, 1987).

64. Henri Nouwen, *Reaching Out*, (Garden City, NY: Image Books, 1966), 66.

65. Hasidic tale quoted in Frederic and Mary Ann Brussat, eds, *Spiritual Literacy* (New York: Scribner, 1996), 502.

66. Dr. Jim Sutherland, *Reconciliation Ministries Network*, Chattanooga, TN. Adapted and used by permission.

67. Ben Vandezande, *Servant Leaders: A Practical Guide for Deacons* (Grand Rapids, MI, CRC Publications, 2000) 15-26. Out of print, used by permission.

PUBLICATIONS

Fort Washington, PA 19034

This book is published by CLC Publications, an outreach of CLC Ministries International. The purpose of CLC is to make evangelical Christian literature available to all nations so that people may come to faith and maturity in the Lord Jesus Christ. We hope this book has been life changing and has enriched your walk with God through the work of the Holy Spirit. If you would like to know more about CLC, we invite you to visit our website:

www.clcusa.org

To know more about the remarkable story of the founding of CLC International we encourage you to read

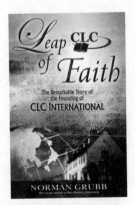

LEAP OF FAITH

Norman Grubb

Paperback
Size 5¹/₄ x 8, Pages 249
ISBN: 978-0-87508-650-7 - $11.99
ISBN (*e-book*): 978-1-61958-055-8 - $9.99

RUNNING ON EMPTY

Jill Briscoe

Feeling burned out? Unfulfilled? Drained? Jill Briscoe offers
hope and comfort for those times in life when we feel empty and
tired. With wit and candor, Briscoe draws lessons from several
biblical figures that provide spiritual refreshment and renewal to
those who are *Running on Empty*.

Paperback
Size 5¹/₄ x 8, Pages 176
ISBN: 978-1-61958-080-0 - $12.99
ISBN (*e-book*): 978-1-61958-081-7 - $9.99

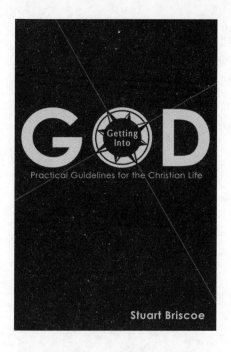

GETTING INTO GOD

Stuart Briscoe

Stuart Briscoe's *Getting Into God* will take you through the basic elements of biblical study, prayer and witnessing. Whether you are a new Christian or one simply wanting to get back to the basics of your faith, this book offers some basic instruction on the "practicalities of Christian experience."

Paperback
Size 5¹/₄ x 8, Pages 144
ISBN: 978-1-61958-152-4 - $11.99
ISBN (*e-book*): 978-1-61958-153-1 - $9.99

GOD ON FIRE

Fred A. Hartley III

As believers, we are more alive in the middle of God's white-hot presence than anywhere else on earth. The history of revival is often studied from man's perspective; what we do to encounter God. *God on Fire* explores what God does to encounter us.

Paperback
Size 5 ¼ x 8, Pages 206
ISBN 978-1-61958-012-1 - $14.99
ISBN (*e-book*) 978-1-61958-066-4 - $9.99

LED TO LEAD

Marty Berglund

Led to Lead challenges ministry leaders to grow deeper in faith through lessons drawn from the life of Moses. This book will challenge you to learn from the life of Israel's greatest leader and to move ahead in your own life and ministry, implementing the lessons learned.

Paperback
Size 5$^1/_4$ x 8, Pages 256
ISBN: 978-1-61958-150-0 - $13.99
ISBN (*e-book*): 978-1-61958-151-7 - $9.99

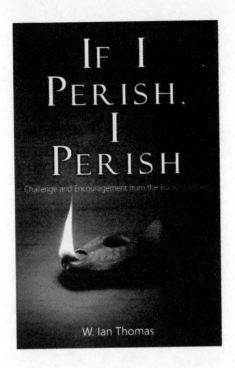

IF I PERISH, I PERISH

W. Ian Thomas

If I Perish, I Perish examines the Christian life through the lens of an allegorical interpretation of the Old Testament book of Esther. The character of Esther, representative of the human spirit, depicts that the call of the Lord Jesus on the Christian is to be crucified with Christ and become alive in the Spirit.

Paperback
Size 4 ¼ x 7, Pages 159
ISBN 978-1-61958-160-9 - $ 9.99
ISBN (*e-book*) 978-1-61958-161-6 - $9.99